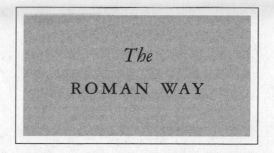

The

ROMAN WAY

BOOKS BY EDITH HAMILTON

The Greek Way
The Roman Way
Three Greek Plays
Mythology
Witness to the Truth
Spokesmen for God
The Echo of Greece
The Ever-Present Past

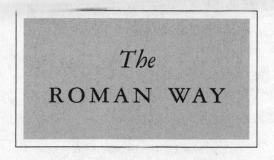

The
ROMAN WAY

Edith Hamilton

W·W· Norton & Company
Independent Publishers Since 1923
New York London

Acknowledgment is made to THEATRE ARTS MONTHLY *for permission to reprint the material in Chapters* II *and* III *which originally appeared in that magazine.*

Published as a Norton paperback 1964, 1984; reissued 1993, 2017
Printed in the United States of America

Manufacturing by LSC Communications Harrisonburg

Library of Congress Cataloging-in-Publication Data
Hamilton, Edith, 1867–1963.
The Roman way / Edith Hamilton.
p. cm.
Includes bibliographical references.
ISBN 978-0-393-31078-8
1. Rome—Civilization.
2. Latin literature—History and
criticism.
I. Title.
DG77.H3   1993
870.9'001—dc20   93–8329
CIP

ISBN 978-0-393-35445-4 pbk.

W. W. Norton & Company, Inc.
500 Fifth Avenue, New York, N.Y. 10110
www.wwnorton.com

W. W. Norton & Company Ltd.
15 Carlisle Street, London W1D 3BS

1 2 3 4 5 6 7 8 9 0

TO

D · F · R ·

—nostrorum sermonum
candide iudex

CONTENTS

PREFACE

If a personal confession may be allowed, although I have read Latin ever since my father, who knew nothing about methods for softening the rigors of study, started me at the age of seven on *Six Weeks' Preparation for Caesar,* I have read it, except during the brief intermission of college, for my own pleasure merely, exactly as I would read French or German. I open a volume of Cicero or Horace or Virgil purely for the enjoyment of what they write, not in the slightest degree because they write in Latin or because they are essential to a knowledge of Roman history. What the Romans did has always interested me much less than what they were, and what the historians have said they were is beyond all comparison less interesting to me than what they themselves said.

It was inevitable, therefore, that when I came to think about the outline of *The Roman Way,* I should see it entirely as it was marked out by the Roman writers. I have considered them alone in writing this book. It is in no sense a history of Rome, but an attempt to show what the Romans were as they appear in their great authors, to set forth the combination of qualities they themselves prove are peculiarly Roman, distinguishing them from the rest of antiquity. A people's literature is the great text-book for real knowledge of them. The writings of the day show the quality of the people as no historical reconstruction can. When we read Anthony Trollope or W. S. Gilbert we get an incomparably better view of what mid-Victorian England was like than any given by the historians. They will always be our best text-books for an understanding of the force back of those years of unparalleled prosperity for the favored few—the character and the outlook of the upper-class Englishman.

That is the kind of text-book I have depended upon exclusively. For each period I have taken only the accounts given by contemporary writers. The contents of the book are the result of a selection based not upon personal preferences but upon how much a writer shows of the life and character of the men of his own times. Plautus and Terence from this point of view are of the greatest importance, as they not only paint the very first picture we have of Rome, but do so in great detail. The century in between Terence and Cicero is, of course, passed over, since none of the writings have survived. Cicero's Rome is taken up at greater length than any other period because his letters are the best source of information we possess for any age, not of Rome only, but of all antiquity.

The force Rome had to mould her people is evident on every page of her literature. All her men of letters were Romans first, individual artists only second. Different, of course, from each other, as Cicero, for instance, is different from Tacitus, or Horace from Juvenal, their differences are yet superficial compared to their fundamental resemblances. During the four centuries which saw the beginning and end of Latin Literature as it has come down to us, every writer shows the main outlines of the Roman way.

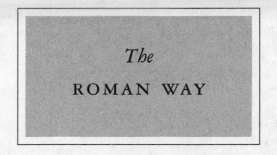

The

ROMAN WAY

I

Comedy's Mirror

When the curtain rings up for the stupendous drama which we know as Ancient Rome, it is raised surprisingly on two comic writers. They are the first to make their appearance on that mighty stage. The oldest piece of Roman literature we have is a collection of comedies. Only two earlier writers are known to us and of their work a few lines is all that is left. Not only Latin literature, but our own direct knowledge of Rome, have their source in comedy, and that not of a rude, popular sort, but sophisticated, a true comedy of manners. The fact, seldom meditated upon, is a little disturbing. We all have our idea of the Romans, implanted by education, by many books: an indomitable people, stern and steadfast and serious beyond all others. It is disconcerting that the fountainhead of our knowledge should be the very reverse of all this. Our notion of the proper beginning for the literature of the mistress of the world would be something martial and stirring, old ballads of valiant men and warlike deeds with spirited bards to sing them, culminating in a great epic, a Latin *Iliad*. But it actually begins as far away from that as the wide realm of letters allows, in a series of comedies which are avowedly founded upon the popular Greek comedy of the day.

No other great national literature goes back to an origin borrowed in all respects. In Greece the development was the natural one, from songs and stories handed down by word of mouth and added to through unknown ages. There was a spontaneous desire in the people—the farmers, shepherds, fighting men—for imaginative expression, which ultimately took literary shape and was preserved. With the Romans it was just the other way about. The literary shape came first, across the sea, from Greece. The desire for expression was secondary, following upon the discovery of an appropriate form ready-made to hand. The fact is full of significance for the Roman mentality.

Roman literature appears suddenly, during the third century B.C., in the generation after the First Punic War, and not only comedy, but everything else as well is modelled upon the Greek. There is hardly even a suggestion anywhere of a native product supplanted by the imported. We find, indeed, a metre never met with elsewhere which the first translator from the Greek used, and a few references in later writers to old ballads heard in boyhood, but that is all. Whether the truth is that the Roman shepherds and farmers, with the strong practical bent that later marked them, had little inclination to spend valuable time in singing songs and making up stories, or whether the literary men when they finally appeared despised the popular productions as beneath the notice of writers who were out to bring culture to Rome and bring it quick, the fact is equally illuminating. A sense for poetry was not strong in the Roman people. Their natural genius did not urge them on to artistic expression. Rome was said to have been founded in the year 753 B.C., and the earliest piece of literature we know about is a translation of the *Odyssey* made at the end of the First Punic War, some five hundred years later. For all these centuries it would seem that the Romans felt little impulsion to express in any form what the world was showing them and life bringing them. Later Roman critics speak of a native comedy, dramatic improvisations at festivals, but there is no warrant for supposing that it was ever written down and it is certain that it had no direct literary descendants.

For us, Roman literature begins with Plautus, writer of comedies after the Greek fashion, and what he shows us of Roman life is the first glimpse we have of Rome. It is a brief glimpse. The curtain raised for him and his successor, Terence, is quickly lowered. When it is raised again we are looking at the age of Cicero.

With the exception of a treatise on agriculture, curiously the one surviving work of the indomitable old censor of morals, Cato, we have only fragmentary bits of the literature in between, no secure basis upon which to reconstruct the city that was already the dominating power in the world. It is true that while Terence, the younger of the two comedians, was producing his plays the Greek Polybius was writing a great history on the rise and growth of the Roman power, of which a considerable part remains, but his concern is with Rome's wars and with the Romans as men of war. The only contemporary information given us about the rest of Roman life up to the first century B.C. comes from the work of the two playwrights.

We may perhaps account ourselves fortunate that comedy was the survivor. There is no better indication of what the people of any period are like than the plays they go to see. Popular drama shows the public quality as nothing else can. But comedy does more. It must present the audience, as tragedy need not, with a picture of life lived as they know it. The comedy of each age holds up a mirror to the people of that age, a mirror that is unique. Ancient comedy, made up for us of four playwrights whose work alone has survived, the Greek Aristophanes and Menander, and the Roman Plautus and Terence, is a mirror where may be seen vividly reflected the Greek and Roman people in periods of notable significance to us: the great day of Greece, an influence still felt in all our thought and our art, together with the age directly succeeding it; the Rome of a hundred years later, when Carthage had been twice defeated and the foundations were solidly laid of the Roman civilization to which our own goes directly back. What we want most of all to know about these two greatest nations of antiquity, is the kind of people that made them up, the every-day men and women, and this history in its concern for wars and laws does not give us. They were the theatre crowd, above all, the comic theatre. It is there we can find them. Popular comedy reflects the average person.

If the Greek tragedians had been lost and we had only Aristophanes left, we should have a very fair idea of the private citizen in Periclean Athens. How little resemblance he had to the theatre-going man elsewhere, what a completely different sort of amusement he wanted, may be seen in every one of Aristophanes' plays. Aristophanes has his own receipt for comedy, unlike, so he himself tells us, all that went before him and certainly never followed by any dramatist since. In choruses of the *Wasps* and the *Peace*, the methods are described which were used by the most popular playwright in Athens to draw his public:

> Your poet in all of his plays has scorned to show you upon
>   the stage
> A few paltry men and their mean little ways. A great
>   theme he gave you—the age.
> He has stripped bare the monster with eyes flaming red,
>   foul vice with its vile perjured band.
> He has battled with spectral shapes, the pains and pangs
>   that are racking our land.[1]

> It was he that indignantly swept from the stage the rabble
>   that cluttered its boards,
> Greedy gods, vagabonds, swindling scamps, whining
>   slaves, sturdy beggars, despicable hordes.
> Such vulgar, contemptible lumber at once he bade from
>   the theatre depart,
> And then like an edifice stately and grand he raised and
>   ennobled the art.
> High thoughts and high language he brought to the stage,
>   a humor exalted and rare,
> Nor stooped with a scurrilous jest to assail some small-
>   man-and-woman affair.[2]

[1] *Wasps*, v. 1027.
[2] *Peace*, v. 739.

Here is clearly written what Aristophanes and his audience wanted from the Comic Muse. In their eyes she was great Comedy, fit to stand beside Tragedy, of equal dignity and with essentially the same deep seriousness. The Old Comedy of Athens stands alone. It is as unlike the comedy of all other countries and periods as the age of Pericles is unlike all others. No small-man-and-woman affair for Aristophanes. Great themes, a grandiose conception of the world, belonged to Comedy, as he saw her, just as much as they did to Tragedy, as Æschylus saw her. That rabble he swept from the stage, those stock characters, each with his fixed form of antics, his thread-bare joke—"a few paltry men and their mean little ways"—gave place to marvelous figures: birds building a city in the sky that put all earthly cities to shame; a band of tight-waisted buzzing wasps to show up the law-courts; radiant Peace in all her beauty; the inexorable world of the dead where art receives its final award. This was Aristophanes' idea of Comedy's province. It died with him and was never found again within the theatre.

The old kind of fun-making came to the fore when he and his audience were gone. That edict of banishment he had proclaimed in great Comedy's name did not hold beyond his lifetime. Back came the exiles, the tricky servant, the braggart, the quack, the drunkard, the cunning thief, familiar stock characters, so his words tell us, four hundred years and more before Christ. The depth of our ignorance about the past is not often so vividly brought to mind. None of that crowded, busy theatre is known to us, nothing of what must often have been brilliant entertainment made by brilliant minds. A marvellous sense for the absurd and a very genius for observing and characterizing human nature put first upon the stage the personages which have held their place there ever since, with the brief exception of Aristophanes' lifetime. Latin comedy and through it all modern comedy have drawn upon the figures of fun unknown Greek playwrights made in the dim past. The small-man-and-woman affair, too, disdained by the great Athenian and his age, took lasting possession not only of the stage, but of literature as well. Aristophanes stands alone indeed. The men who fought at Salamis and planned the Acropolis and carved the Parthenon sculptures gave the laws to the Athenian drama, and when they died there was no audience any more for great Tragedy and great Comedy.

Athens, we are always told, was a democracy, based, of course, upon slavery because that was the pre-requisite to civilized life in the ancient world, but except for that, a place where all men were free and politically equal. But there are democracies and democracies. The Periclean pattern was not like that which succeeded it. There is a marked difference between a young and a full-grown democracy. In the first, aristocracy still lingers. Aristocratic standards are abroad. The democracy of Washington at Mt. Vernon wears another look from that of Mr. Coolidge in Vermont. Pericles was an aristocratic democrat and there is an extremely qualified democracy in Plato's young men. The theatre audiences of that day were people of highly cultivated tastes who could not be amused with the commonplace. But fourth century Athens was another matter. The aristocrats were gone and democracy was in secure possession. There was no need of fighting and suffering in its behalf. Athens was comfortable and undistinguished; life was lived on an easy middle-class level. The New Comedy, one ancient writer after another assures us, reflected the age, in especial the chief ornament and exponent of the innovation, Menander. An enthusiastic Alexandrian exclaims: "O Life, O Menander, which of you two was the plagiarist?"

Of all his fellow artists he alone has survived, but only in small part. No complete play has come down to us. Indeed, up to a few years ago he was directly known through short extracts merely, lines cited to illustrate some point, and the like. Indirectly, however, much was deduced from the unqualified praise and devoted imitation of him by ancient critics and writers. But the discovery of nearly the whole of one play and considerable portions of several others has made it dubious how far that great reputation was deserved. They are pleasantly written, these plays, the characters not infrequently drawn with skilful and delicate touches, the dialogue occasionally entertaining, the plot contrived with some ingenuity, but more than that cannot be said of them at their best and at their worst they are very dull indeed. They are not funny. They are little dramas of little folk; a miniature art done in very quiet tones; subdued pictures of a well-to-do, completely commonplace society, showing the bad punished and the good rewarded, but moderately as the vices and virtues are moderate, and always a happy marriage to bring down the curtain. What would Aristophanes have made of them, one wonders. There is not the faintest reminiscence of his soaring imagination, not the most distant echo of his roaring laughter. The difference between the two playwrights illumines as nothing could better the change that had come over the Athenians in the space of hardly fifty years.

That brief flowering of genius, the golden age not of Greece alone but of all our western world, had been brought about by a lofty and exultant spirit, conscious of heroic deeds done and full of joyous courage for great enterprises to come. It had lived in the audiences who shouted at Aristophanes' riotous nonsense, who delighted in every brilliant bit of his satire, appreciated each delicate parody, with minds keen to follow his master mind. But the flame, so intense, so white-hot, quickly sank, leaving behind only a comfortable fireside warmth. Menander's audiences wanted nothing in the very least Aristophanic. They were out for pleasant, unexciting entertainment, reassuringly like their every-day life, and, above all, guaranteed to make no demands upon the intelligence. Comfort, prosperity, safety, was the order of the new day that produced the New Comedy. Under their soothing influence the Athenians changed so swiftly they were themselves surprised and seeking for a cause laid it to Sparta's account. The world ever since has echoed them, but to read Menander is to

understand perfectly how inevitable was the passing of the Periclean age, to perceive other far more potent causes than the victory of Sparta in the Peloponnesian War.

In Rome, comedy has an even greater significance for us. The
two Roman comedians are immensely important, beyond the
Greek even from one point of view, in that they made the actual
models upon which European comedy formed itself. With them
we enter the great sphere of Latin influence, mighty in moulding
our civilization, direct and all-penetrating as never was that of
Greece. Aristophanes founded no school. He had no followers,
ancient or modern. Menander has lived only as a shadow in
Roman plays. Plautus and Terence were the founders of the drama
as we know it today.

But how far they hold up comedy's mirror to the life of their
own times is a matter not easily determined. As has been said,
they are all the literature of that period which we possess. There
is not one contemporary record by which their credibility can be
tested as a source of information about Rome. The question how
closely they imitated the Greek New Comedy, to what degree
they translated or followed their own genius, is one to delight the
scholarly mind because it never can be settled by scholarly standards. The battle of the learned can be waged forever. Too little is
left of Menander's work for even the most erudite to give the victory on that score to either side, and of his fellow-comedians nothing is left at all. However, the absence of clear-cut facts, with
which alone the scholars are really concerned, is not fatal to the
argument. In deciding the matter there are certain general aspects
of the question which cannot be passed over and they tell conclu-
sively for the originality of the two Romans.

Their own evidence in all they say about their work is strongly
in favor of Menander. Their prologues give the names of the
Greek plays, Menander's or one of his school, upon which they
declare their own are modelled. Neither man ever lays claim to
originality beyond the trifling degree involved in making occa-

sionally one play out of two. In one of Terence's prologues he quite plumes himself on having translated a certain incident word for word. But on this point it must be remembered that in antiquity a copyist, far from being thought less of, was highly esteemed if he copied what was known to be good. Plautus and Terence would have every motive to emphasize their connection with the admired Menander. And against this evidence there is a consideration so weighty, it turns the scale decisively in favor of the plays being a veritable Roman product: the essential quality of a comic play.

Those who argue that they gave their audiences not Rome but Greece, foreign folk whose ways were strange to Romans, do not take into account the nature of comedy. It must present the familiar. An easy understanding of what is going on is essential. Let puzzlement or what follows inevitably in its train, disapproval, come in and comedy is at an end. The audience are not there to have their minds enlarged geographically or ethnologically. They want to see people they know about and life lived in the way they live it. A stray foreigner acting according to his own foolish foreign notions is a capital figure of fun, but a stage peopled with such would not be funny at all. In one of Plautus' plays a slave is rewarded for good service by being given a cask of wine and permission to entertain his friends. The feast that follows was essential to the plot of the Greek original so that Plautus could not leave it out, but he knew that it would seem strange to his hearers, indeed quite shocking to their ideas of how slaves should be treated, and he makes the slave turn to the audience and say: "Don't you be surprised that slaves drink, court, give invitations to dinner. That is allowed us at Athens." Plautus' instinct as a comedian was sure. He would not have his actors out of touch with his public. But this is the only occasion when he feels an explanation necessary.

The people who laughed at these plays were on terms of friendly intimacy with their characters and found nothing "foreign" in their ways. Those who hold to the contrary might as well argue that Antipholus and Dromio, whose originals are in a play by Plautus, are Romans—or Greeks—and not Elizabethans. Shakespeare would never have attempted to people his plays with Romans. *The Comedy of Errors* has no more to do with Rome—or with Ephesus—than *A Midsummer-Night's Dream* has to do with Athens. The English stamp is upon the two Dromios just as clearly as upon Bottom and his crew. *Les Fourberies de Scapin* follows Terence's *Phormio* so closely in many scenes that occasionally the dialogue is a direct translation, but Molière would never have fallen into the fatal mistake of making his personages anything but French. As Molière well knew, comedy's range does not reach beyond the national frontier—not even in our own age of Internationalism. Every continental comedy transported to us today must suffer a change on the way to make it acceptable to Americans.

It is true that both the Romans always state that the scene of their comedies is a Greek city, just as the names of the characters are Greek, but the fact has really no bearing at all upon the argument. There was an excellent reason for that convention which had nothing to do with the nationality of the people of the plays. It was of great practical importance for a Roman comedian to choose a far country for his fun. The stage has always been a most attractive field for legislators, and the Romans, who had a very passion for passing laws about everything in the world, revelled in the censorship. A law of the Twelve Tables condemned people to be whipped who wrote anything defamatory, and one of Plautus' contemporaries had been imprisoned and then exiled—a punishment only less terrible than death in those days—for writing a play in which there was a single disrespectful allusion to dignitaries. Back of this procedure was a fixed idea about what a Roman citizen must be. A kind of divinity hedged him in and no scurrilous playwright was to make him ridiculous. Faced with this dilemma, comedy a matter of fun but no fun to be made of Romans, the comedians sensibly turned to foreign parts for their scenery. Further than that they did not trouble themselves. These people with Greek names walk in the forum, go to the capital, worship the Roman household gods, allude contemptuously to "those Greeks," and so on. To be consistent was not important, but to escape the censor was.

Political allusions, too, would have been equally dangerous. Nothing really is more inconceivable than Aristophanes at Rome. The Roman formula of condemnation when a man had done ill by the state, was: *For diminishing the Majesty of the Republic.* The fate of that arch-diminisher of majesties would have been so swift in Rome, he would never have written a second comedy. The thought has significance for Plautus at least. Something in his rollicking, jovial spirit, his exuberant vitality, recalls though ever so faintly the Old Comedy. It is not hard to imagine his turning those shrewd, twinkling eyes of his upon public as well as private follies and giving us a picture of the Rome of statesmen and politicians and great affairs, which would make it live in some sort as Athens lives in Aristophanes. But the Roman way was far from the Greek way. A free stage or anything else free was not for Romans. Order, well enforced by magistrates, was the Roman idea.

Theories that go counter to the facts of human nature are foredoomed. Comedy in Rome to be comedy had of necessity to be Roman and no argument, linguistical, historical, archæological, can have any counterbalancing weight against this fundamental truth. The mirror of Plautus and Terence reflects not a strange, shadowy Greece, but their own day and their own city, the veritable Rome of the Republic.

Ancient Rome Reflected in Plautus and Terence

Roman comedy plays the same rôle that all comedy everywhere plays. It takes us behind the scenes of history's stately drama. In Plautus' mirror the curious may see how that austere figure fixed in our minds from early schoolroom days, the Ancient Roman, appeared to view when he was out to be amused.

What do the words Republican Rome call to mind? Discipline, first and foremost, then frugality, hardihood; white-toga-ed figures of an incomparable dignity; ranks of fighting men drilled to the last degree of military precision; an aura of the simple life lived, not quite on heroic heights, but at any rate on perpetual battle-fields; Cincinnatus at the plough; the death of a son decreed by a father for disobedience of orders even though a victory resulted. That is the sort of thing we think of as early Rome. This edifying picture is considerably enlarged and diversified by Roman comedy. In Plautus we get the reverse of the shield, the senator not in his toga but in the Roman equivalent of dressing-gown and slippers; the soldier dispensing alike with armour and discipline; dignity, iron resolution, the stern compulsion of duty, the entire arsenal of the antique Roman virtues, completely in the discard.

In the *Merchant*, one of Plautus' most entertaining plays, a young fellow, sent on a business trip by his father, bought a lovely lady while away and has just landed bringing her back with him. As he comes on the stage his slave enters running, breathless, able only to gasp out: "Terrible—dreadful—awful—awful news–Oh, it's bad, bad."

MASTER: (*after repeated petition for something clear*) * Speak
    it out. What *is* the matter? Don't dare say bad news
    again.

SLAVE: Oh, don't ask me. It's too awful.

MASTER: By the Lord, you'll be so thrashed—

SLAVE: If I must, I must. Your father—

MASTER: (*terrified*)   Father! What?

SLAVE: He saw the girl.

MASTER: Hell! How could he?

SLAVE: With his eyes.

MASTER: But how, you fool?

SLAVE: By opening 'em.

MASTER: Damn you. Quibbling when my life's at stake.

SLAVE: Oh, cheer up. Worse to come. Soon's he saw
    her the old blackguard started petting.

---

   * In the following translation, as in all others, the text has been condensed.
Very few plays lend themselves to quotation. The actors are essential, and
rightly so, to any real appreciation of them. But even more than most, Roman
comedy would be wronged by a word for word rendering. These plays afford
excellent scope for an actor, but they move slowly for a reader. To give the passages as they stand would mean to lose the point completely in any citation
brief enough to be included here. In each case the metre of the original has been
reproduced.

MASTER: Heavens! Her?

SLAVE: (*snorting*) Strange it wasn't me—

> (*The two young men go off to try to get the girl safely away, and the father enters with a friend of his own age, his next door neighbor.*)

FATHER: (*very sprightly*) Come, how old d'you think I look?

FRIEND: (*dispassionately, looking him over*) Decrepit. One foot in the grave.

FATHER: (*dashed for a moment, then recovering*) Oh, your eyesight's failing. I'm a boy, old friend—not eight years old.

FRIEND: Are you daft? Oh—second childhood. Yes, I quite agree.

FATHER: No, no. (*archly*) I've begun to go to school, old man—four letters learned today.

FRIEND: Eh? Four letters?

FATHER: LOVE

FRIEND: (*surveying him unsympathetically*) You in love with that gray head?

> (*turning to audience*) If you ever saw a portrait of a lover there he is.
> The old dotard—feeble, tottering. A nice picture you'll agree.

*(Appealed to for old acquaintance' sake, however, he agrees
to go to the ship and buy the girl for his friend, and offers
until the other can find a place for her, to take her to his
own house, as his wife is away. In the next act he enters
with the girl, who seems much agitated.)*

FRIEND: Come along, my girl. Don't cry. Don't spoil those
pretty eyes of yours.

GIRL: *(sobbing)* Do be nice to me and tell me—

FRIEND: There, there. Just be a good girl
And you'll see a good time's coming.

GIRL: Oh, dear, dear. Poor little me.

FRIEND: How's that?

GIRL: Where I come from it's the naughty girls that have
the fun.

FRIEND: That's to say there are no good ones?

GIRL: No, indeed. I never say
Things that everybody knows.

FRIEND: *(beginning to think she is far too nice for the old fool
            next door)* By Jove, the girl's a perfect pearl.
Worth more than she cost to hear her talk. Well, come
my beauty, now.
Into the house with you quickly.

GIRL: So I will, you dear old thing.

The selection could be duplicated over and over again. Plautus loves the senator in his lighter moments. An equal favorite is the soldier. In the first scene of his *Braggart Captain* the captain enters with an attendant, Artotrogus, and several orderlies carrying an enormous shield.

CAPTAIN: (*strutting back and forth*, ARTOTROGUS *at his heels,*
          mimicking him)
    Make ye my buckler's sheen outshine the radiant sun
    To dazzle in the fray the myriad hosts that seek me.
    Now do I pity this poor blade (*drawing his sword*) that
        idle hangs
    When so it longs to slash to bloody shreds my foes.
    Artotrogus!

ARTOTROGUS: (*popping out with a wink at the orderlies*)
    Here, sir, beside our warrior bold.
    Oh what a hero!

CAPTAIN: (*wrapped in great memories*) Who was he—that
    man I saved—

ARTOTROGUS: The time you puffed the foe away as with a
    breath?

CAPTAIN: A trifle really—a mere nothing, that, to me.

ARTOTROGUS: Indeed, sir, yes, compared with other feats I
    know
    (*Aside*) You never did. (*Aloud*) In India that elephant—
    My word, sir, how you smashed his foreleg into pulp
    Just with your fist.

CAPTAIN: Oh that? A careless tap, no more.

ARTOTROGUS: Oh, sir, that other day too when you nearly
  killed
Five hundred at one stroke.

CAPTAIN: Ah, yes, mere infantry.
  Poor beggars—so I let them live.

ARTOTROGUS: Oh, unsurpassed!
  And all the women mad about you, simply mad.
  Those two girls yesterday—

CAPTAIN: (*very careless*)   What did they talk about?

ARTOTROGUS: About you, sir, of course. Says one, Is he
  Archilles?
  Says I, His brother. Oh, the other says, That's why
  He looks so noble. And then didn't both of them
  Beg me to lead you past their house like a parade,
  To feast their eyes on.

CAPTAIN: (*yawning*)   It's a real affliction to me
  To be so handsome.

Such is the appearance of the Father of the State, in history's
sober pages the pillar of the Republic's Majesty, and of the martial
ancestor of Caesar's legions, when they are presented in their
lighter aspects, from what might be called the point of view of the
home. The domestic drama, which is essentially the drama as we
know it today, has its direct origin in these Latin plays. The intimate domesticity of family life in one of its most impressive man-
ifestations, the Roman family, is the pivot they all turn on, and
character after character is shown which the theatre has never let
go of since. Here is the very first appearance upon the world's
stage of the figure so dear to audiences everywhere, the Mother,

essentially what she is to be through all the centuries down to our own with the white carnation and Mother's Day. Greece never knew her. The Mother, capitalized, was foreign to Greek ideas. But the Romans in such matters were just like ourselves and often more so. One of Terence's good young men, finding on his return from a journey that his newly married wife has gone back to her father's house presumably because of a quarrel with her mother-in-law, is instantly aware of what he should do:

> Since she thinks it's not for her to give in to my
>   mother's ways,
> Says her self-respect won't let her, it seems clear I've got
>   to choose,
> Either leave my wife, or mother. A son's duty must
>   come first.

> FATHER: Right, my boy. Your mother first. There's noth-
>   ing you should put ahead.

The father has a place even more prominent. What they called in Rome the *Patria Potestas*, the Father's Authority, was clearly an awful matter. There was no rebelling against it. In Plautus' *Comedy of Asses* a father, much taken with a girl his son is in love with, is sitting at table beside her, very jovial. The son, very mournful, sits opposite:

> FATHER: Come, my boy, you don't mind, do you, if she
>   sits 'longside o' me?

> SON: (*dolefully*) I'm your son. I know my duty, father. I'll
>   not say a word.

> FATHER: Young men must be modest, son.

SON: Oh, yes, I know. Do what you want.

FATHER: (*briskly*) Well, fill up—good wine, good talk. No
    filial awe, my boy, for me.
    It's your love I want.

SON: (*more doleful*)   Of course, I give you both as a son
    should.

FATHER: I'll believe it when you take that look off.

SON: Father, I am sad.
    It isn't that I don't wish everything you wish. You know
    I do.
    But I really love her. Any other girl I wouldn't mind.

FATHER: But it happens I want this one. Come, tomorrow
    she'll be yours.
    That's not much for me to ask.

SON: (*wretchedness complete*) You know I want to please you
    first.

But the authority of the master of the house had its limits.
Plautus' Rome was the Rome of the Mother of the Gracchi and it
is not difficult to understand that the Roman *Pater Familias*,
weightily endowed though he was by law and edict and tradition,
might meet his match in the determined virtues of the Roman
matron. Indeed that resolute lady seems to be responsible for the
creation of one of the most popular characters in literature, the
hen-pecked husband. He makes his very first bow upon the stage
in these plays.

His sufferings give Plautus great delight. In the *Merchant*, a
wife returning unexpectedly from a visit in the country finds a

very questionable young person very much at home in her house.
She runs out proclaiming her wrongs.

> WIFE: Oh, never was a woman so abused as I,
>   Or never will be. Married to a man like that—
>   And I who brought him two good thousand pounds in
>   gold.
>
>   *(Husband enters. Stops and eyes her in great alarm)*
>
> WIFE: Such insults. Bring that creature to my house—
>
> HUSBAND: Ye Gods!
>   I'm in for it. She's seen her.
>
> WIFE: Heaven help me now!
>
> HUSBAND: (*feelingly*) Oh, no. Me, me. I'd better speak to
>   her—My dear,
>   You're back? So soon? Well, this is pleasant.
>
> WIFE: Who's the girl?
>
> HUSBAND: (*tentatively*) You saw her?
>
> WIFE: Yes, I did.
>
> HUSBAND: Well, she's—oh, she's—oh, damn.
>
> WIFE: You're stuck.
>
> HUSBAND: (*sulkily*)   The way you keep at me.
>
> WIFE: Of course, it's I.

No fault of yours. (*with change of voice*) I've caught you in
   the act. That girl—
Say who she is.

HUSBAND: (*aside*)   Oh, this is all too much for me.

In such scenes, of course, the end is always that he is reduced
to the state of a helpless victim while she triumphs. "Mayn't I
even have my dinner first?" one of them pleads when his wife
appears to drag him home from the party. "I'll see you get the dinner you deserve," is her answer, and he follows her unprotestingly.
"I kept telling you, father, you'd better not try any tricks on
mother," the son says smugly as the slaves bring in the food. And
with the contrast between the gay dinner table and the dark door-
way through which "mother" relentlessly drives "father" the play
ends. Perhaps the most familiar passage in Virgil is the one in
which he bids the men of Rome remember that to them belongs
the rule of the earth. They are to "spare the submissive and war
down the proud." It would seem that this high charge was subject
to modifications within the home.

The plays leave no possibility of doubt that although public
life was denied the Roman woman, she could find a very fair out-
let for her energy in the domestic circle. In Plautus' *Casina*, a representative of the character Plautus is perhaps fondest of, the true
ancestor of Pantaloon, is in love with his wife's protégée and plans
to have his bailiff marry her and then give her over to him. The
wife counterplans with her maid to dress up the footman as the
bride and take a spectacular vengeance. The maid opens the scene.
She comes out from the house in high glee.

MAID: No games, I don't care where, not even the
   Olympic,
Are half the sport the joke we're playing our old man.
He's bustling in and out in such a mighty hurry.

And there's the bailiff all rigged up, so spick and span,
And mistress in her room is dressing up—the footman!
And oh, the lovely way she does pretend—They're here!

(Enter old man. He speaks through door to his wife)

OLD MAN: I'll take the bride and groom out to the farm.
  It's safest.
Enjoy yourself here. I'll dine there. But hurry, please,
And send them out. Until tomorrow then, my dear.

(Enter footman dressed and veiled as bride, wife and maid escorting him)

MAID: Now, do be gentle with this innocent young girl.

BAILIFF: Indeed I will.

OLD MAN: Go in. *(nervously as the door shuts)* My wife—is she still there?

BAILIFF: She's gone.

OLD MAN: *(dancing excitedly around bride)* Hurrah! Oh, sweetheart, honey, flower of spring—

(They go off, and some time is supposed to have passed before the next scene, which discovers wife and maid waiting for the result of the instructions given the footman.)

MAID: *(tittering)* I'd like to see that bride and bridegroom now, I would.

WIFE: I'd like to see the old scamp's face well battered in.

*(They draw back as the old man enters, much dishevelled,
tunic torn, all the signs of rough handling.)*

OLD MAN: I don't know how I'll ever face my wife again.
But there—In I must go and pay her damages.
(to audience) Would one of you here like to substitute for
me?
(Pauses a moment, then shakes his head) I just can't stick
it.

(Makes as if to run when enter footman)

FOOTMAN: Stop right where you are, old man.
(coyly) Now if you want to fondle me, sir, here's your
chance.

WIFE: *(stepping out, followed by maid)* Good day to you,
young lover.

MAID: *(joining in)*   How did your courting go?

FOOTMAN: *(sobbing)* He doesn't love me any more.

OLD MAN: Wish I was dead—

The entire scene could have been played just as it stands by any
commedia dell' arte troupe. Not a character there that would not
have been perfectly familiar to actors and spectators.

But there is one notable difference between what an audience
would accept from women in Plautus' day and in later times. The
deceived husband, so familiar for so many centuries to the European stage, never appears in Roman comedy. There is no indication of any other bar to the activity of the Roman wife, but she
could not put horns upon her husband's head. No Puritan moral-

ity could be more unyielding on this point. The fact is thrown into high relief by the complete absence of any sex-morality in other directions. The courtesans are important characters in nearly every play and Terence's most estimable youths have affairs with them which their mothers on occasion hotly defend. One of his irreproachable young men, passionately in love with such a lady, agrees to share the possession of her with a blustering bully in order that his own purse may be spared. Familiar characters, too, are the panderer or his female equivalent. In Plautus' *Comedy of Asses* a lover is raging up and down before a house where doors and windows are all conspicuously closed:

LOVER: Thrown out of doors! That's the reward I get
For all I've spent upon them. You'll be sorry.
I'm off to the police—leave your names with 'em.
I'll humble you, your girl too—

(Enter MADAM *from house, very calm and pleasant)*

MADAM: Go right on threatening. Such a state of mind
Means money down. Get off. Away with you.
The more you try, the quicker you'll come back.

LOVER: And all I've given you! If I could have her
Just for myself now, why you'd owe me sums.

MADAM: *(cheerfully)* Oh, you can always have her—on condition
You give what's asked—and more than other men.

LOVER: Be just a little kind. I'll last you longer.

MADAM: *(coolly)* You miss the point. A lover's like a fish
Where we're concerned—no good unless he's fresh.

Your sweet, fresh, juicy ones—ah, they're the men.
They don't care what it costs. They *want* to give.
To please their girl they'll give to me, the servants.
Make up even to my little dog. Now come—(*reasonably*)
A woman's got to look out for herself.

Such passages, side by side with the idea steadily presented throughout the plays of a sacrosanct family life, throw a flood of light on the kind and the degree of morality abroad in the Republic. The Romans were franker than our grandfathers were, but their basic notions of what could and could not be done were the same. Strict virtue within the house for everyone. Outside, all the pleasant vices for the men. A hard and fast division of ethics into male and female received its final consummation in Rome. The double standard which has been the world's standard for all these centuries since, is formulated, complete to the last detail, in Roman comedy. In this respect the men of Greece were dull of wit compared with the men of Rome. Their astuteness did not rise beyond the four walls of the house for their women folk, with occasional assistance from bolts and bars, most futile of defenses, as story-tellers the world over have shown. Aristophanes has many a joke about the way Athenian women eluded them and the husbands they deceived. Nothing of the kind passed with a Roman audience of the Republic. The men saw to it that they were not deceived, and the way they did it was a triumph of Roman intelligence as well as of Roman determination. One of Rome's greatest achievements, which has passed almost unnoticed, was the successful education of their women in the idea that their supreme duty was to be chaste. The popular story of Lucretia who killed herself when she was violated by force, completely innocent though she was in reality, and the story, even more popular, of the father acclaimed a hero because he killed his daughter with his own hand rather than have her live as the tyrant's mistress, testify eloquently to the thoroughness of the women's training. Thus disciplined they were safe to go abroad and enjoyed a degree of freedom civilized women had never known before. But the lesson was taught so cleverly, the idea that men's pleasures, too, should be curtailed never entered the women's minds. Their conviction of the all-importance of chastity, side by side with the conviction that it had nothing to do with men, is a proof of what the Roman mentality could accomplish when faced with a practical problem.

The whole matter bears directly upon the Roman character of the plays. Plautus' women, who have so influenced the women of all later drama, were never drawn from Greek originals. In the *Amphitryon*, Alcumena is the model Roman matron complete, and the line of her descendants upon the stage is too long to be reckoned. On her—supposed—husband's departure for the war she soliloquizes in words which recall all the soliloquies spoken by noble women the world over when the necessities of the drama require them to be abandoned by their lawful protectors:

> Absent from me
>   So let him be,
> If fame and glory come
> With him triumphant home.
> Bear and forbear,
> Make my heart strong,
> Through bitter care,
> Days sad and long,
> All this I can endure, all and yet more,
> If I may hear him hailed at last victor in war.
>   That prize enough for me.
>   His valor's prize shall be
>   Mine. What is all the rest?
>   Valor is best.
> *(As she concludes, Amphitryon, her real husband, enters.*
> *The circumstances are complicated: Jupiter has been assuming*
> *Amphitryon's form while the latter is away fighting, and*

*has thus gained access to Alcumena with whom he is in love.
It is he Alcumena has just taken leave of. Upon Amphitryon's unexpected return, Jupiter has decamped, telling her he
is due at headquarters. When Amphitryon enters she, of
course, thinks they parted only a few moments ago. In this
delicate situation she is the perfect Roman lady, indeed, the
perfect lady of every age and clime.)*

AMPHITRYON: (*entering eagerly, followed by his slave*) Joyfully
    I greet my wife, my own, my hope, the very best,
So her husband thinks, of all the ladies that the city
    holds.
    You are well? Glad I am come?

ALCUMENA: Oh dear. Please don't. I hate such jokes.
    Why pretend we haven't met before?

AMPHITRYON: We haven't!

ALCUMENA: (*not condescending to notice this*)   Back so soon?
    Weather? Bad news? Or what's the cause? You told
    me you were due in camp.

AMPHITRYON: Told you? When?

ALCUMENA: Why keep on teasing? When? Some
    time ago—just now.

AMPHITRYON: (*to slave*) Why, she's raving.

SLAVE: She's asleep.

ALCUMENA: I? What's this nonsense?

AMPHITRYON: Greet me, dear.

ALCUMENA: Yesterday I greeted you.

AMPHITRYON: When we made harbor just last night!

ALCUMENA: Nonsense. You were here last night and told
    me all about the war.
  Here we dined and slept together.

AMPHITRYON: O my God!

ALCUMENA: What do you mean?

AMPHITRYON: She has had her lover here. She's lost—
    seduced—my wife no more.

ALCUMENA: Sir, you neither know me nor my family. Take
    care. You will find
  We are not that sort of people.

AMPHITRYON: You are bold.

ALCUMENA: No, innocent.
  The real dowry that I brought you was not gold but
      purity,
  Honor, self-control and reverence for the gods, my par-
      ents too,
  Love to all my kin, obedience to my husband, serving
      him
  In true faithfulness.

AMPHITRYON: My word, I'm so dazed I don't know
    myself.

Madam, I'll investigate the matter.

ALCUMENA.   Dear me, Do, I beg.

Talk like this is so familiar to us, it is difficult for us to realize how new it was in the second century before Christ. It bears the true Roman stamp. There is nothing like it in Greek literature. Conscious virtue, noble declamation, a fine gesture—none of that is Greek. Where the Romans were all for exalted sentiments, the Greeks were singularly matter-of-fact, and this difference is an important reason, perhaps the chief reason, why we feel instinctively at home in the Roman way and strangers to the Greek. A certain amount of heroics is necessary for us.

Another point in this passage which is new to the student of Greek literature is the exaltation of woman and her purity. That, too, began in Rome. Greek tragedy, indeed, shows women of a greatness unsurpassed anywhere. The greatest figures are women, but the fact that it is so is never directly brought to mind. We are never made to feel, how wonderful that a woman should be like that, any more than, how wonderful that a man should be. Antigone and Iphigenia are as they are, just as Œdipus and Orestes are as they are. The sex is as little to the fore in the one case as in the other. But in Roman literature, as in our own, a woman is always a woman. Her sex is never in the background of the picture.

The idea, too, which our literature for hundreds of years has made familiar to us, that she is on a higher plane than any man has reason to be, goes back to Rome. It resulted, of course, from the insistence that chastity was strictly for women only.

Roman sentimentality, also, appeals to us, just as the lack of it in Greek literature repels us. Along with the comedy there is invariably in Terence and often in Plautus a love interest, a pair of unhappy lovers, whose troubles find a perfect solution as the curtain falls. The girl is always a model of beauty and virtue, the young man madly in love with her. They are never touched by any of the indecencies the other characters may indulge in; they are never humorous. The Roman audience wanted both sides: greedy courtesans and easily-tricked panderers and senile dotards to laugh at; good, sweet young people to sympathize with.

But the character that stands out first of all, far beyond even the dominating figures of the father and the expensive lady, is the slave. He is the ancestor of all the devoted and agile servitors, models of fidelity and never fazed by any of their masters' difficulties, whom literature everywhere has made so familiar, but in Rome the rôle he played was more important than any given him since. The portrait of the Roman family would lack its chief feature without the slave and no Roman comedy could be written without him. In every play he is the chief personage, the only one with brains, who succeeds in fooling all of the people all of the time. But in spite of his gay assurance and his triumphant success, his terrible lot in Rome is continually suggested. One of Terence's characters, represented as loveliest and kindest of ladies, offers her maid-servants for examination by torture to prove her innocence. The punishments the slaves are perpetually threatened with might well have given points to the inquisitors, and, obviously, the reason for the detailed descriptions is that they were delightfully humorous to the audience. The cross—the slave's penalty, they called it in Rome—is often on the master's lips. Sometimes, but only once or twice, there is a hint as to the slave's side. In Plautus' *Braggart Captain* a master is denouncing his slave, who in this case is innocent. As the list of tortures in wait for him is unrolled he turns on the speaker:

> Don't go on threatening. Well I know the cross will be my
>   end,
> My place of burial. There is where my ancestors all rest,
> My father, my grandfather, and my great-grandfather, too.
> My great-great grandfather. D'you think just words mean
>   much to us?

It is difficult to understand how the hearers could have laughed at this and yet we must suppose they did. No doubt at all, the tide of human kindness, never high anywhere in the ancient world, ebbed perceptibly when Rome came to the fore, but on the other hand the actual suffering of the slave is very seldom shown upon the stage and the end is always that he is forgiven and rewarded. The enjoyment from the spectacle of actual danger to life and limb the Romans of the day reserved for the circus shows. They did not care for it in the theatre.

On the whole, the general impression the plays leave is that they were written for fairly decent, sober-living folk, completely moral within their homes and even outside wanting nothing decadent. The obscenity is moderate judged by Aristophanic standards. There is a genuine feeling, too, for justice and fair play, and vice and virtue must always have their deserts. Once only Plautus fails to live up to this ideal and at the end of a play shows two bad old men enjoying themselves with two girls who had begun by making fun of their white hairs. The curtain falls on their triumph, but Plautus knew his public and was ready with an antidote. There is an epilogue holding up to reprobation all the elderly who act like that. Terence never had to apologize for his endings. He assigns rewards and punishments with impeccable correctness.

It is a world far removed from Elia's "land of Cuckoldry, the Utopia of gallantry, where pleasure is duty and manners perfect freedom." No fancy roams in it, whether to Utopia or anywhere else; gallantry is undreamed of; freedom is equally remote; pleasure, of the physical variety alone. It is a sordid place, inhabited by people whose standards are at best those of a dull respectability, whose ideas are completely ordinary, not to say stodgy. There is no suggestion of distinction or charm anywhere. Terence, to be sure, shows now and again a flash of insight, as in his famous "I am a man and nothing in mankind do I hold alien to me." The younger comedian was intellectually superior to the elder, but even so the flashes are few. Terence's world, too, lies on the dead level of the commonplace.

Fragments of Menander have come down to us which show that neither he nor his audience had quite forgotten the great Greek tradition:

> I hold him happiest
> Who before going quickly whence he came,
> Hath looked ungrieving on these majesties,
> The world-wide sun, the stars, water and clouds
> And fire. Hast thou a hundred years to live or but
> The briefest space, these thou canst always see.
> Thou wilt not ever see a greater thing.

There is not a passage in Plautus or Terence that recalls ever so faintly anything like this, not one that points to something poetical in their model, however dimly apprehended. A single sentence of Plautus', perhaps, should be excepted; at any rate it gives one pause, it is so strangely unlike the self he shows elsewhere:

> The poet seeks what is nowhere in all the world,
> And yet—somewhere—he finds it.

Did he himself occasionally wander away from this actual, solid world, one wonders, and was it his audience that held his plays so fast down to it?

A good-humored crowd, those people who filled the Roman theatre in its first days of popularity, easily appealed to by any sentimental interest, eager to have the wicked punished—but not too severely—and the good live happily ever after. No occasions wanted for intellectual exertion, no wit or deft malice; fun such as could be passively enjoyed, broad with a flavor of obscenity. Most marked characteristic of all, a love of mediocrity, a complete satisfaction with the average. The people who applauded these plays wanted nothing bigger than their own small selves. They were democratic.

That audience of two thousand one hundred years ago looks oddly familiar. The reflection shown in the mirror of Plautus and Terence has "nothing alien" to us as we watch it. The close family life and the masterful lady of the house and the elderly-man-in-search-of-a-mistress and the nice young lovers—we know them all only too well and we cannot feel ourselves strangers to the theatre-crowd that flocked to see them in Rome of the Republic.

A Roman comedy 200 B.C., a Broadway musical comedy, 1932 A.D.—the gulf between can be passed without exertion. Save in respect of time only, it is neither wide nor deep. This swiftly changing world we must all run so hard to keep up with suddenly looks strangely static.

III

The Comic Spirit in Plautus and Terence

Plautus and Terence, as has been pointed out, are the founders of our theatre. Their influence has been incalculable. The two main divisions of comedy under which all comic plays except Aristophanes' can be grouped, go back to the two Roman playwrights. Plautus is the source for one, Terence for the other. The fact is another and a vivid illustration of how little the material of literature matters, and how much the way the material is treated. Both dramatists deal with exactly the same sort of life and exactly the same sort of people. The characters in the plays of the one are duplicated in the plays of the other, and in both the background is the family life of the day, and yet Plautus' world of comedy is another place from Terence's world. The two men were completely unlike, so much so that it is difficult to conceive of either viewing a play of the other with any complacency. Plautus would have been bored by Terence, Terence offended by Plautus. Precisely the same material, but a totally different point of view, and the result, two distinct types of comedy.

Plautus was the older by a generation. His life fell during a restless period when Rome was fighting even more than usual. He could have taken part in the Second Punic War and the wars in the east which followed it, but whether he did or not is pure conjecture. All that is actually known about him is that he was the son of a poor Umbrian farmer, that he worked once in a mill and wrote three of his plays there, and that he was an old man when he died in 184 B.C. But it is impossible to read him without getting a vivid impression of the man himself. A picture emerges, done in bold strokes and unshaded colors, of a jovial, devil-may-care vagabond, a Latin Villon; a soldier of fortune who had roamed the world hobnobbing with all manner of men, and had no illusions about any of them; a man of careless good humor, keen to see and delighting to laugh at follies, but with a large and indulgent tolerance for every kind of fool.

Terence was a man of quite another order. He was born a slave in one of Rome's African colonies and brought up in a great Roman house where they recognized his talents, educated and freed him. These talents, too, found him a place in a little circle of young men who were the intelligentsia and the gilded youth of Rome combined. The leader was the young Scipio, but the elegant Laelius, no mean poet, and the brilliant Lucilius, the inventor of satire, were close seconds, and it was an astonishing triumph that the former slave, once admitted, proved inferior to none of them. It requires no imagination to realize his pride and happiness at being made one of their number. When envious people declared that his grand friends wrote his plays for him, he answered proudly that he boasted of their help.

It was a very youthful company. Terence is said to have died before he was twenty-six and they were all much of an age. The plays show nothing more clearly than that the audience they were primarily written for was this little band of close friends and not the vulgar crowd. Every one is laid in the Utopia of a young man about town in Republican Rome. Undoubtedly the members of the group in their bringing up had had a great deal required of them in the way of the antique Roman virtues. The father and mother of the day, as Plautus shows them, were not given to overindulgence, and Scipio Africanus Maior, the young Scipio's grandfather by adoption, must have been a man very much to be reckoned with in the family circle, while the ladies of the Scipio household were notable for their practice of the domestic virtues. The redoubtable Cornelia herself was his aunt and her jewels were his cousins. No doubt at all he and his friends had had to walk a narrow path with watchful guardians on either side.

But under Terence's guidance, art, the liberator, set them free. He took them away to an enchanted world where fathers were what they ought to be and young men had their proper position in the world. Plautus' fathers were hard on their sons and—more intolerable still—the young fellows were held up to ridicule. Terence altered all this delightfully. For the most part his fathers are of an amiability not to be surpassed. "Does my darling son want that pretty flute girl? The dear boy—I'll buy her for him at once." "Extravagant do you call him? Well, all young men are like that. I was myself. I'll gladly pay his debts." There is never any joking at that sort of thing. Such sentiments are the part of a right-minded man. Indeed, there are no jokes at all where the young men are concerned. They are all wonderfully serious and completely noble and accorded the deepest respect. Plautus' young lover on his knees before the door that shuts in his lady-love, undoubtedly moved the audience to laughter when he declaimed:

> Hear me, ye bolts, ye bolts. Gladly I greet you, I love you.
> Humbly I pray you, beseech you, kneel here before you to
>   beg you,
> Grant to a lover his longing, sweetest bolts, fairest and
>   kindest.
> Spring now like ballet-girls dancing, lift yourselves up
>   from the door-post.
> Open, oh open and send her, send her to me ere my life
>   blood
> Drains from me wasting with waiting.

But who would laugh at Terence's estimable young man, so admirably concerned for his love:

> I treat her so? And she through me be wronged, made
>   wretched,
> She who has trusted love and life, her all, to me?
> So will I never do.

They are all like that. Whatever the audience thought of them, they were certainly not amused. But whereas Plautus was out to get a laugh by any and every means possible, Terence had an entirely different object in view. Plautus talked directly to the spectators when the action failed to get a response, calling out to the man in the back row not to be so slow to see a joke, or to the women in front to stop chattering and let their husbands listen, or making an actor warn another,

> Softly now, speak softly.
> Don't disturb the pleasant slumbers of the audience
>   I beg.

His object was to amuse. But Terence's mind was bent upon the approval of what he thought the most fastidious, polished people that ever there had been, and he worshipped where they did, at the shrine ever dearest to youth, good taste, as laid down by the canons of each youthful circle, "the thing," which is and isn't "done." Plautus makes fun of everyone, gods included. Terence has few comic characters, and they are in general confined to the lower classes. One catches a glimpse of an English public-school feeling for good form in that little circle of serious young men of which he was so proud a member. Making gentlemen ridiculous was simply not "done." Fortunately, in the circumstances, Terence's sense of humor was such that it could be perfectly controlled. No doubt to him Plautus was a terrible bounder—Plautus, the comedian pure and simple, who when he is not funny, is nothing at all. Terence is a serious dramatist, able to write an amusing scene; but seldom choosing to do so. His interest is in his nice people, above all his nice young men, and in their very well-bred-man-of-the-world doings. It is not to be presumed that Plautus knew anything about well-bred men, and no one ever had less concern for good taste. His quality is Rabelaisian—diluted—and certainly he would have been as much disconcerted by Terence's fine friends as they would have been uncomfortable with him.

With dissimilarities so marked it is not surprising that they disagreed about the whole business of drama-making. The fundamental question of how to secure dramatic interest each solved in his own way, completely unlike the other's. They constructed their plays differently and two forms of comedy, widely divergent from each other, were the result.

There are only two main sources for dramatic interest in a comedy. The first is the method of suspense and surprise, depending upon plot or upon the reaction of character to character, or to situation. But the second method is precisely the reverse: it acts by eliminating suspense and making surprise impossible. The dramatic interest depends upon the spectators knowing everything beforehand. They know what the actor does not. It is a method found in both tragedy and comedy; it is common ground to the sublime and the ridiculous. The Greeks who made great use of it, called it irony. Nothing in tragedy is more tragic. Œdipus invokes an awful curse upon the murderer of his wife's first husband:

> I charge you all: Let no one of this land
> Give shelter to him. Bar him from your homes,
> A thing defiled, companioned by pollution.
> And solemnly I pray, may he who killed,
> Wear out his life in evil, being evil.

And we know it is he himself he is cursing, he is the murderer; he killed his father, he married his mother. This is tragic irony. It lies at the very foundation of Greek tragedy. The audience knew beforehand what the action of each play would be. They sat as beings from another world, foreseeing all the dire results of every deed as it took place, but perceiving also that thus it must be and not otherwise. The feeling of the inevitability of what is being done and suffered upon the stage, of men's helplessness to avert their destiny, which is the peculiar power of Greek tragedy, depends in the last analysis upon irony, upon the spectators' awareness and the actors' unconsciousness of what is really happening. The darkness that envelops mortal life, our utter ignorance of what confronts us and our blinded eyes that cannot see the ruin we are bringing down upon ourselves, is driven home so dramatically and with such intensity as is possible to no other method.

The use of it may be as comic as it is tragic. We, the audience, are in the secret that there are two men who look exactly alike. The poor, stupid actors do not dream that it is so. How absurdly unable they are to escape their ridiculous mishaps, and what a delightfully superior position our omniscience assures to us.

We cannot trace back the use of the suspense method. Plot is as old as the very first story-teller and the interest of what the effect will be of a situation or of one character upon another is at least as old as Homer and the Bible. But irony begins with Greek tragedy, and, as far as our evidence goes, comic irony begins with Roman comedy. Among the fragments we have of Menander there are two in which irony is evident, but in neither passage is it used humorously. It is found so used for the first time in Plautus. If he was indeed the originator of it, if it was he who perceived to what comic uses tragic irony could be turned, he deserves a place in literature far higher than that now given him. Irony is his chief source of dramatic interest and he is a master of it. It follows, of course, that he offers nothing notable in plots. Suspense is automatically shut out when irony is used. Plautus' plots, when he has one, are extremely poor, and there is a distressing similarity between them. But no one ever put irony to better comic use. His usual way is to explain the action of the piece in a very long and exceedingly tiresome prologue, but the result of the detailed explanation is that the spectators are free to give their entire attention to the absurdities they are now in a position to see through.

In the *Amphitryon*, it will be remembered, Jupiter is in love with Amphitryon's wife, Alcumena. When Amphitryon is away at war Jupiter assumes his form to gain access to Alcumena. Mercury, who guards the house whenever Jupiter is in it, under the form of Amphitryon's slave, Sosia, absent with his master, speaks the prologue, and explains in minutest detail all that is going to take place throughout the play. Jupiter and Amphitryon will look exactly alike, he warns the audience, and so will he and Sosia, but in order that they may have no bother as to which is which, Jupiter will have a bright gold tassel hanging from his hat and

> I shall wear this little plume on mine,
> Note well: the other two are unadorned.

With this the play begins. The scene is a street at night before Amphitryon's house where Mercury stands on guard. To him enters his duplicate, Sosia, sent ahead by Amphitryon to prepare his wife for his unexpected return. It is too dark for Sosia to see how Mercury looks. As he goes up to the door the latter stops him.

MERCURY: May I know where you come from, who you
    are, and why you're here? Just you tell me.

SOSIA: Well, I'm going in there. I'm the master's slave. Do
    you know it all now? Just you tell me.

MERCURY: Is that your house?

SOSIA: Haven't I said so?

MERCURY: Then who is the man that owns you?

SOSIA: Amphitryon. General commanding the troops. He's got a wife—name Alcumena.

MERCURY: What stuff are you giving me? What's your name?

SOSIA: It's Sosia. My father was Davus.

MERCURY: Well, you've got your cheek. You're Sosia? You? What's your game? Didn't know I was he? Eh? (*Strikes him.*)

SOSIA: Oh, you'll kill me!

MERCURY: You'll find if you keep this up there are things a whole lot worse than dying. Now, say who you are.

SOSIA: I'm Sosia, please—

MERCURY: He's mad.

SOSIA: I'm not. Why, you rascal. Didn't a ship bring me in from the battlefield this very night? Didn't my master Send me here to our house? And you say I'm not—Well, I'll go straight in to my mistress.

MERCURY: Every word a lie—I'm Amphitryon's slave. We stormed the enemy's city, Killed the king—cut his head off, Amphitryon did.

SOSIA: (*awestruck*) He knows it all. (*pause, then recovering*)
   Just you tell me
   If you are me, when the fight was on, where were you?
   What were you doing?

MERCURY: A cask full of wine in the tent and my own
   pocket flask.
   What d'you think I'd be doing?

SOSIA: (*overwhelmed*) It's the truth. Wretched man that I
   am.
   (*shakes head, then suddenly holds lantern up so that the
   light falls on* MERCURY)
                Well, well. He's as like me as I myself was.
   Oh, immortal gods! When was I changed? Did I die?
   Have I lost my memory?
   Did they leave me behind in foreign parts? I'm going
   straight back to my master.

   (*Runs off, and re-enters following* AMPHITRYON *who is completely nonplussed at the report of what has happened.*)

AMPHITRYON: (*angrily*) The boy's drunk. You, speak up.
   Tell the truth, where you got the stuff.

SOSIA: But I didn't.

AMPHITRYON: (*uneasiness getting the better of his anger*)
   Who's that man you saw?

SOSIA: I've told you ten times. I'm there at the house
   and I'm here, too.
   That's the straight truth.

AMPHITRYON: (*trying to persuade himself it's all nonsense, but
      uncomfortable*)   Get out. Take yourself off. You're
      sick.

SOSIA: I'm just as well as you are.

AMPHITRYON: Ah, I'll see that you aren't. If you're not
      mad, you're bad.

SOSIA: (*tearfully*)   I tell the truth. You won't hear me.
      I was standing there in front of the house before I got
      there.

AMPHITRYON: You're dreaming.
      That's the cause of this nonsense. Wake up.

SOSIA: No, no. I don't sleep when you give me an
      order.
      I was wide awake then—I'm wide awake now. I was
      wide awake when he beat me.
      He was wide awake too. I'll tell you that.

AMPHITRYON: (*gruffly*)   It'll bear looking into. Come
      on then.

This is the way Plautus handles comic irony. Molière follows him
closely. In his *Amphitryon* the dialogue between Mercure and Sosie
is essentially a reproduction of the Latin and no one can say that
the great master of comedy used the device at any point more
skillfully than the Latin poet.

      Playwright after playwright took it over from him. Shake-
speare's ironical play, *The Comedy of Errors*, is not as close a parallel
to Plautus' *Menaechmi* as Molière's is to the *Amphitryon*, but the

entire play is only a variation on Plautus' theme. Scenes in Shakespeare and Molière where the comedy depends upon irony are so
many, to run through them would mean making a résumé of a
large part of their comedies. The basis of the fun in *Much Ado
About Nothing* is the spectators' knowledge of the plot against
Beatrice and Benedick. The great scene in *L'Avare* is funny
because we know the miser is talking about his money box and
the young man about his lady-love, while each supposes the other
has the same object in mind. Here, too, Molière drew directly
from Plautus. Whether the latter first employed the method or
whether he got it from the Greek New Comedy, it is certain that
its use upon our own stage goes directly back to him.

Terence never used it. It seems strange at first sight that he did
not, but upon consideration reasons appear. A plot intricate
enough to supply a full measure of suspense and surprise can be
enjoyed only by an intelligent and attentive audience, especially
when programmes, outlines, synopses of scenes, all the sources of
printed information, have to be dispensed with. Plautus' audience
was not up to that level; Terence's was—the real audience he
wrote for, his little circle of superior people. Plautus had to hold
the attention of a holiday crowd, and hold it too, as he says in
many a prologue, against such competitors as chattering women
and crying babies. No method of playwriting requires so little
effort on the part of the spectator as comic irony. Comedies based
upon it are merely a succession of funny scenes strung on the
thread of a familiar story. There was sound sense in Plautus' pref-
erence for it, and equally good reason for Terence's rejection. His
audience enjoyed using their minds on an ingenious plot. He
could dispense with the obviously comic and follow his own
strong bent toward character and situation. The germ of the novel
lies within his plays. His plots are never poor. Perhaps the best of
them is that of the *Mother-in-Law*, where the suspense is excellently sustained to the very end. Indeed, as the curtain falls the
two chief characters pledge each other to keep the solution of the

mystery to their own selves. "Don't let's have it like the comedies where everyone knows everything," one of them says.

It is a good story throughout and the characters are well drawn. Nevertheless when the play was presented to the public it failed. The prologue, spoken at a second presentation, declares the reason was that

A rope-dancer had caught the gaping people's mind.

Yet another prologue—for still another presentation, presumably—says that the theatre was thrown into an uproar by the announcement of a gladiatorial show, and the play could not proceed. Clearly the road of the early dramatist in Rome was not an easy one, but there is never a hint that Plautus found it hard. Perhaps he had the happy faculty of not taking himself too seriously, and merely went along with the crowd when such occasions worked havoc with his play. One feels sure that even so he would have enjoyed the rope-dancer. But the young playwright, hardly more than a boy, felt poignantly the hurt to his feelings and the wrong to his genius. Every one of his prologues contains an attack upon his critics or his public. They are fearfully serious productions, warranted to make any audience restless and any other show irresistibly attractive, but to his own inner circle, those very sober and cultured young men, no doubt they appeared admirably distinguished from the well-worn, old-fashioned method of appeal to the vulgar.

The marked difference between the two writers is another proof of the Roman character of Roman comedy. Plautus and Terence owed something, no doubt, much perhaps, to their Greek originals, but much more to their own selves. They were Roman writers, not Greek copyists, and the drama they bequeathed to the world which still holds the stage today, is a witness to the extent of our legacy from Rome.

IV

Cicero's Rome

The Republic

While Terence was writing his plays a very remarkable man came to Rome. He did not come voluntarily; he was brought there as a hostage and there he had to stay for seventeen years. In all that length of time the city grew to be a home to him instead of a prison, and after he was released he came back again for another long stay. He was Polybius, the Greek historian, and except for Plautus and Terence, what he has to say about Rome is the only contemporary record before Cicero which has come down to us. He was a man of great ability, a true scientist in his love of truth, a keen observer of human affairs, qualified as few could be more to weigh the good and the bad in the great city which even then he saw as the coming mistress of the world. His testimony is overwhelmingly in her favor. He has a profound admiration for the Republic and for the Roman character. To be sure, his keen eyes saw signs of moral weakening after Carthage was conquered; even so, his history is a great testimonial to the city he knew through and through, to Roman uprightness and patriotism, and to the Roman mastery of the art of ruling men.

He was not a flatterer, trying to win for himself the favor of a powerful nation. When he wrote he was an old man, living far from Rome in his early Greek home. He dared to praise Hannibal, to blame Rome sharply for more than one breach of faith. If the government had been corrupt, he would certainly have known it and certainly recorded it. He never so much as hints at such a condition. His Romans are simple and hardy in ways of life, upright, steadfast, devotedly and disinterestedly patriotic.

But an enormous change has taken place when next we have a contemporary's account of the city; the government is corrupt through and through and the people completely indifferent. Only a hundred years—less than that—changed Polybius' great Republic into one of which we have as black a picture as could well be painted. Indeed, to the historian Sallust, a man with something of Polybius' passion for accuracy, the change was fully consummated a generation earlier. A foreign prince, so he tells the story, came to Rome at the beginning of the first century to engineer a deal. He was rich and he succeeded, and as he left the town he said, "City in which everything is for sale."

That is the city shown in the next authentic record of Rome. It is a remarkable record. During the strange and exciting days when the great Republic was coming to an end and the Empire was looming just ahead, there lived the most distinguished letter-writer the world has ever known, one of Rome's very great men, Cicero the orator.

Hundreds of his letters have been preserved, along with many letters from his friends. They are of all sorts: letters of condolence, letters of affection, letters of apology, literary criticism, philosophical discussion, town gossip, business letters, and, outnumbering all the rest a hundred to one, political letters. Such a ratio would be a matter of course to a Roman. The thing of paramount importance, away beyond everything else, was politics. Throughout the great days of the Republic it had been the field both of duty and honor. A good man, a great man—both terms were synonymous with a patriotic man. Goodness apart from patriotism did not exist to the Roman. All the men who counted, whether by birth or property, had been brought up in the tradition that they were bound to be politicians first; whatever else they might take up must be treated as of secondary importance. Our letter-writer in any other age would have had no leanings toward politics. He belonged by nature to the men of thought, not of action. He was a student, a lover of books, a critic and a man of artistic tastes, too, the very last sort of person in our eyes to enter public life. Rome made him into a politician, so devoted to his calling that when events removed him from it he was inconsolable. What of comfort could philosophy, literature, art, give to a Roman forced to lead a private life? Cicero was disgraced and contemptible in his own eyes.

That was the conception which had enabled the Republic to endure for hundreds of years perpetually encompassed by unnumbered perils. The best brains, the strongest characters, had always been at the absolute disposal of the state. Her service had been at once their chief obligation and their greatest joy.

A wonderful help in ensuring brave men and men capable of self-sacrifice to manage state affairs was the fact that politics and war were inextricably connected. Any day a successful politician might find himself compelled to desert his constituency, don his armor, and march against a foe whose forces outnumbered his own. The practice of politics in Republican Rome had never been for those in search of an easy berth. It was ever a dangerous pursuit. The odds were that favors voted by the people would have to be paid for on the battlefield.

It would have been unthinkable to a Roman that high personal courage was not an essential part of the equipment of a politician. Officials, party chiefs, "bosses" big and little, must face an ever present possibility of having to die for their country. Ex-officials were allowed no more comfortable prospects. Consulars, as they called them, men who had been consuls—Rome's ex-presidents— became oftenest commanders in the wars Rome was always waging in one or another part of the world. Cicero, pre-eminently a man of peace, sensitive in the extreme and timid, a lover of ease and luxury, in his fastidious culture a typical man of letters, must yet put himself at the head of an army and live for months at a time as a fighting general. It was the price he paid for once having been placed at the head of the state. In none of the many letters he wrote from the seat of war is there a word of complaint against the fate that carried him away from his beloved city and his books and the comforts of his country houses and his pleasant ways of life, to far distant Cilicia and the hardships of a guerilla war. He was merely doing what he had expected when he came forward as candidate for the consulship.

The high distinction which always attends the fighting forces of a nation at war marked out the Roman politician as well, the distinction which only conspicuous danger and death can give.

And yet when Cicero was carrying on his Cilician campaign in strict accordance with Rome's great tradition, the Republic was dying and all but dead. That was in 51 B.C. Nine years before, three powerful party leaders had come together; they agreed to pool their resources and take the government into their own hands. But it was all completely unofficial and no one need take cognizance of it if he chose not. The senate met; the consuls presided; the old respected political forms were strictly adhered to. The fact that Caesar, Pompey, and Crassus held the reins did not seem to matter much, if they kept, as they did, in the background. People got used to the idea of them and when four years later their powerful organization was completed and they began to act openly, honored and honorable patriots could find excellent reasons for acquiescing in their running the city. Indeed, it seemed exceedingly probable that if they did not do so there would be nobody to run it. As regards the senate, once and through so many centuries Rome's great guide, the only question that could be raised was whether it was more incompetent than it was corrupt or the other way about. Something had happened to Roman morale. The people were safe and at ease. Rome's enemies were outside Italy now, far away, shut off by mountains or sea, and although civilian commanders were the rule, fighting in other respects had become a matter for professionals. Wealth was pouring into the city from conquered countries; easy money had become possible for a great many and the ideal for most. To have three able men take the responsibility of looking after Rome's wide interests saved a vast deal of trouble for others. The old

Republic had exacted a great deal from her citizens and left them poor. Now people wanted politics at a profit; they were out for a share in the riches they saw around them.

Politics have seldom offered a better field for that purpose than they did then. Rome had in very truth become the city where everything was for sale. Cicero's letters make it possible to see the inwardness of the political situation clearly as in hardly any other period of history. Bribery here, there and everywhere, he writes over and over again, not an official exempt, not even the highest. Politics have become a money-making business; votes are bought and sold, so are judges. Everyone knows that there is one sure way to being elected or being acquitted, and nobody cares. One day, Cicero writes, there was read out in the senate an agreement a candidate for the consulship had made with the two consuls to pay each of them a large sum of money in case he was elected, but failed to get for them the offices they wanted when their term was over. The compact called for false oaths not only from the principals but from two ex-consuls as well. "It was regularly drawn up," Cicero continues, "with the sums promised, and drafts on the bank added, and so on. It does throw a lurid light on the consuls, but it was all the same to Appius Claudius [one of them]—he had nothing to lose by it."

The reason for that remark was that in the eyes of all Rome no Claudius had anything left to keep or lose in the way of reputation. Once the Claudii had been citizens Rome was proud of. The Appian Way was the achievement of an ancestor; so was the first water system, and the splendid aqueduct. They had been great people and no house was more aristocratic. The present representatives, however, were not of the antique stamp. Appius, his brother Publius, and their three sisters, all noted for brilliancy and personal beauty, were talked of throughout the city for their reckless ways, their extravagance, dissipation, and worse. There was nothing so bad that Rome was not ready to whisper about them and believe. The *cause célèbre* of that day and many a day to come centered in Publius, and Caesar's young wife, Pompeia, was co-respondent.

As Cicero tells the story it is a cynical drama of corrupt politics. It began at the festival of the Good Goddess, a highly important ceremony in which women alone took part. During the celebration no male could enter the house where it was held. The master must find other lodgings; even pictures and statues of men were banished. Juvenal says no male mouse dared to stay. Caesar was pontifex maximus at the time and his house was chosen for the sacred rite. This suited Clodius, as Cicero always writes the name, exceedingly well. His affair with Pompeia was not coming off, Plutarch thinks because of the strict chaperonage of her mother-in-law, "a very discreet woman," and here was an occasion when the most vigilant duenna might relax. His smooth boyish beauty fitted well a woman's dress and he arranged with Pompeia to go to the house disguised as a singing girl and be met at the door by her own maid. No doubt the dare-devil adventure urged him on quite as much as his passion. The maid was on hand as he entered and bidding him wait slipped away to find her mistress. But she was long in coming back and Clodius, who, to be sure, was never one to wait patiently for anything, started to find his lady for himself. But something had gone wrong. Perhaps Pompeia's courage failed; more probably the very discreet woman had had her suspicions aroused, for as he went through the house her maid ran up to him and called out gaily that he must come and play with her, a custom, Plutarch says, at the festival—it would be pleasant to know what they played at—and upon his drawing back, asked him what was wrong. Clodius had the folly, inconceivable on the part of anyone except his arrogant, reckless self, to speak to her in answer and his voice betrayed him. She shrieked, "A man—a man!" and the fat was in the fire. Great was the to-do. The "sacred things" were covered; the holy rites pronounced null and void; the house ransacked. To no purpose, however; Clodius had been smuggled out by Pompeia's maid. All the same, he had been recognized and of course next morning the town buzzed with the delightfully horrific scandal.

The women made the most of it. A tribune was found to impeach the offender for profaning sacred ordinances, and a number of husbands were persuaded to bring forward in addition to this clearly substantiated charge, another which every Roman lady had shuddered at and passed on to her friends, but which obviously could not be clearly substantiated, that he had committed incest with one of his sisters, or indeed, with all three. Clodius contented himself with declaring that he was out of town at the time of the festival and had witnesses to prove it. Caesar put the best face he could on the matter: swore he did not believe a word of it; Clodius had never been in the house; a lot of women's talk. It was true he divorced Pompeia, but then he was ready with a reason which commended itself to every masculine heart, voiced in the famous saying about Caesar's wife.

Clodius, we may well believe, enjoyed himself. A trial for sacrilege was certain, but he knew the way out from that. Cicero was drawn into the affair. He was in a position to testify that Clodius had been in town, for he had called to see him the very evening of the festival. Rumor had it that he was extremely reluctant to move in the matter and that the reason was the lovely Clodia, the most beautiful and notorious of the three sisters. It is certain that he often speaks of her in his letters, and his nickname for her, "our ox-eyed goddess"—elsewhere he mentions her great flashing eyes—would point to some intimacy. At all events, Cicero's wife, a lady built on the lines of Plautus' Roman matrons, laid down an ultimatum and Cicero came forward as the chief witness for the prosecution. The enmity he aroused thereby followed him implacably through his life and even after. It was the part of a wise man to avoid giving offense to people like the Claudii, and the supple politician that lived in Cicero along with several widely divergent characters, was perfectly aware of the fact—but then there was Terentia, a violent lady, says Plutarch.

One of Cicero's letters gives a full account of the proceedings: "If you want to know about the trial, the result of it was incredible. The challenging of the jury took place amidst an uproar, since the prosecutor, like a good censor, rejected the knaves, and the defendant, like a kind-hearted trainer of gladiators, set aside all the respectable people. When the jury finally took their seats, a more disreputable lot never got together even in a gambling hall. All the same, these noble talesmen declared that they would not come to court without a guard [in a previous letter Cicero says that Clodius has several gangs of ruffians at his command]. No one thought Clodius would even defend his case.

"'Tell me now, ye Muses, how first the fire fell.' Well, Baldpate [Cicero's name for Crassus, the richest man in Rome] managed the whole job in a couple of days with the help of just one slave. He sent for everybody, made promises, gave security, paid money down. Some of the jury were even presented with the time—at night—of certain ladies, and some with introductions to young men of good family. Even so, five and twenty of them were brave enough to prefer to risk their lives, but thirty-one were more influenced by famine than fame. Catulus meeting one of them later remarked, 'Why did you ask for a guard? For fear of having your pocket picked?' There you have the trial in brief and the reason for the acquittal. But I was the man who revived the fainting courage of patriots. I was speaking before the Senate soon after and by a happy inspiration I introduced into my speech this passage: You are mistaken, Clodius. The jury saved you for the gallows, not for public life. Keep up your heart, senators. We have merely discovered an evil that existed unnoticed. The trial of one villain has revealed many as guilty as himself. But there, I've nearly copied the whole speech for you. Up gets the pretty boy and reproaches me with spending my time at Baiae [as we should say at night clubs or at Monte Carlo]. It was a lie and anyhow what did it matter? 'You've bought a house,' he says. 'You seem to think it's the same as buying a jury,' I answer. 'They did not credit you on your oath,' he retorts. To which I answer, 'Twenty-five credited me. The other thirty-one gave you no credit but took care to get their money first.' Loud applause and he collapsed."

Yes, but nothing happened. Well-meaning citizens would applaud, but when it came to doing anything that meant personal effort, not to say inconvenience and even possible danger, that was another matter. Not long after this impressive demonstration of patriotic feeling, Clodius was elected to high office.

To the modern reader of the record it seems incredible that anyone, let alone those shrewd, competent Romans, should have believed that such a state of things could go on and on and a republic in which no one trusted either the electorate or the courts could in the nature of things endure. But so it was. Not even Cicero, superman that he was, read the handwriting on the wall. To be sure, he is perpetually saying that this or that piece of perfidy has dealt a death-wound to the state, but he never for a moment believes it. The laws are disregarded; the courts are despised; armed gangs face each other in the forum; the elections are a farce; the man with the largest purse always gets in, and nobody cares. Why should they? Life goes on most comfortably and agreeably in the great city, more so by far than ever in the world before. A violent change in government or in anything else is inconceivable. Business is good; great fortunes are made quickly in the provinces; at home it is not hard to keep the rank and file contented. Citizens of a republic where every man has a vote have easy ways open to them for getting money, and even wide-spread unemployment, when it occurs, no longer threatens danger. The people are kept contented not only by cheap food but also by the Roman equivalent of free tickets to the theatres and the major league games. Let the courts and the Big Three carry on as they like; nothing is really important but a pleasant, easy life which sensible people can have if they choose. Cicero, during a temporary lapse of his ruling passion, writes his brother: "Anything more corrupt than the men and times of today cannot be conceived. And so since no pleasure can be got of politics, I don't see why I should fret myself. I find my pleasures in literature and my favorite pursuits and the leisure of my country houses and, most of all, in our boys."

Ten years after that letter was written the Republic was ended; Antony and Augustus were dividing between them the Roman world; Cicero's headless body was lying on the seashore. In one of his letters he says that it is easy to know how to pull the ropes in a bad cause, but hard in a good cause, and "it is a difficult art to rule a republic."

V

Cicero Himself

Of most famous people we know only the imposing façade. We have no key to open the door and let us enter. Cicero belongs to the very few who have left the key behind.

The general outline of what he did is familiar to us all: he was one of the two greatest orators of antiquity and everything else about him is in comparison negligible. This is the traditional idea of him, and from one point of view it is quite true. Today, after two thousand years, there are speeches of his which still live; the roll of their grand periods can still stir an emotion, and nothing else that he wrote has this power of independent life. His treatises, his politics, philosophy, rhetoric, have gone the way of all the books that decorate the library and are never read. And yet, even so, they have a claim upon the world's respect and admiration: few writings have had as many and as devoted readers. To run through the most famous of them now, the essay on Old Age, on Friendship, is to feel the impatience a perpetual mental "Of course" always awakens, but once these truisms were strangely new and it was Cicero who made them common. For centuries he was the main channel by which Greek standards reached mankind. He had the power so to write them down that people everywhere read and believed them. He harnessed Greek thought to his heavy Roman car and the huge shapeless mass of men Rome was to form to civilized ways, caught a glimpse of what would else have soared far above them.

This achievement hardly needs illustration; it is acknowl-

CICERO HIMSELF 69

edged. Also, quotations of truisms are less enlightening than boring. Yet a few may perhaps be permitted. Some remembrance is
due to the standards Cicero set, the effect he had upon this stubborn world. The gentleman, the English gentleman, who has
meant much to many generations, may well have had his beginning in, certainly he was fostered by, the English schoolboys'
strenuous drilling in Cicero. Our orator knew a great deal about
the matter—which is not to say that he always lived up to his
knowledge. His orations are not specimens of gentlemanly
restraint, but there he followed, as he was bound to do, the customs of the courts. In his letters, where he is really himself, he
always shows a perfect good breeding.

The fundamental precept of the gentleman, that if in a bargain
one of the parties is to come out worsted, he must be the one, is
laid down uncompromisingly in one of his essays. Liberality in
spending, too, he knew was part of the code; he is firm against
economy that might be a cover for meanness. In political matters
if gentlemen take different sides, there can be no heat of contro-
versy between them, however burning the question; they are well-
bred men first and always, politicians and opponents second. And
never, under any provocation, must a gentleman (N.B., *not* a
lawyer) allow himself to refer to his antagonist's private life. Such
points of conduct rank with the most important in his eyes.
Among the terrible charges he brings against Mark Antony in the
Second Philippic is the one of violating the gentleman's code: "He
has quoted openly a letter he said I once wrote him! What man
knowing even a little the ways of honorable men, ever because of
some later offence, quoted a letter written by one who was at that
time a friend?" Words like these were seeds in fruitful soil when
they became part of the Englishman's education.

To teach mankind so effectively that the teacher ceases to be
needed because the lessons have permanently affected men's fundamental convictions, is a very great achievement. Nevertheless it
is a second-rate achievement. The greatest writers do not enter

into the general consciousness and then cease to be. We cannot
drain them dry and pass on, revived but never called back to find
refreshment there. They belong in the city which was built

> to music, therefore never built at all,
> and therefore built forever.

Plato does not merely fill a shelf in our libraries. But Cicero is
the man in Plato's parable of the poet who cannot be admitted to
the temple, "being uninspired and having no touch of madness in
his soul." In his greatest orations, there is fire. When he pleaded
for unfortunate men or the unfortunate Republic—to him the
most precious thing on earth, he writes a friend—he had passion
and the power to put it into great words. But in the austere
regions of the impersonal it failed and died.

He was not a typical Roman, but he had the training given all
Romans by the most practical and efficient city the world had
ever seen or was to see for two thousand years, and the undivided
mind which thought demands was not only never his, he did not
want it. He wanted to be doing something and if in a crowd, so
much the better. Alone, unoccupied, he was bored. "I am so
driven from pillar to post I can hardly find time for these few lines
and even that I must snatch from important matters." The surface
complaint does not conceal the deep satisfaction. In all the letters
from Rome this tired-business-man attitude is to the fore, and in
the country, in one of his delightful villas, the case is hardly better: "Writing is impossible. My house is a public hall, it is so
crowded with the village people. Of course, the small fry don't
bother me after ten o'clock, but Arrius lives next door, or, more
truly, with me. On the other side is Sebosus!" In the next letter:
"Just as I was writing these words in comes Sebosus and I had
hardly time to sigh when there was Arrius saying good morning.
This is going out of town!" All the same, when the bores spare
him and leisure enfolds him, the result is not happier and cer-

tainly the letters are duller. "Nothing could be pleasanter than this solitude. All is more charming than you can imagine, the shore, the sea view, the hillocks, and everything. But they don't deserve a longer letter—and I have nothing else to say—and I am very sleepy—." Something more exciting than nature and meditation was necessary to keep Cicero awake. He wanted the movement of the great world; he wanted political life and a foremost part in it.

He achieved his ambition: he was the most important man in Rome when he put down Catiline's conspiracy, and for nearly twenty years he fought in the vanguard of all the political fighting, a great figure, thundering denunciations in the forum, pleading with passion against injustice, firing a feeble senate to stand by the state, a devoted republican, a patriot of the antique Roman stamp.

That is the façade, stately, imposing: and if it were not for his letters that is all we should see, as it is all we see of the heroes of history everywhere. But of these many letters, which number over eight hundred, more than half are written to a man with whom he was on terms of closest intimacy. He had nothing to hide from Atticus; with him he put up no pretense; he was content to appear just what he was. In his letters to other friends he remembered and would have them remember that he was one of Rome's leading men, moved, as Rome's leaders had ever been, by loftiest motives. To them he is sure that "only the honorable is the truly profitable," that "true worth is always victorious," that "nothing is expedient but what is right," but he never writes in this strain to Atticus. With him he is completely at ease. He can talk as he wants about everything and make jokes of matters he would feel bound in writing anyone else to take with decorous solemnity.

Of the letters Atticus wrote Cicero not a single one has been preserved and the so-called life of Atticus which has come down is hardly more than a long-drawn encomium. It is known, however, that he kept his large property intact through all the political convulsions of the times, and that he lived to be an old man, in those days quite as signal a triumph of worldly wisdom, and with the added light thrown by Cicero's correspondence he stands out clearly, a cool-headed man of business, whose standards were the expedient and the profitable and who made it comfortable for people to dispense with all pretensions to any other standards in his company. "There is no one, not even myself, with whom I talk as freely as with you," Cicero writes him. With this key Cicero unlocked his heart and the contents lie open for inspection.

He tells him that his son-in-law has been left property by a lady; he is to share with two others a third of her estate, but upon condition that he change his name. "It's a nice point," is Cicero's cheerful comment, "if it's the right thing for a noble to change his name under a woman's will—but we can decide that more scientifically when we know how much a third of a third amounts to."

He sets down with complete candor what many have felt and few been willing to say: "When I write you praising any of your friends I do wish you would let them know. I mentioned lately in a letter Varro's kindness to me and you answered you were glad to hear it. But I had much rather you had written him that he was doing all I wished—not that he was, but to make him do it."

His oratorical effects—"the mature outcome of my talent, the finished product of my industry," when he speaks of them to others—to Atticus become delightfully something to poke fun at: "All that purple patch I so often use to decorate my speeches—the passage about fire and sword. You know the paints I have on my pallet. Ye Gods, how I showed off! You know how I can thunder. This time it was so loud I expect you heard it right over there."

When he must come to terms with Caesar whom he hated and had denounced over and over again as the destroyer of everything good in the state, he can find very fine words to dress up his motives for other friends: "To speak of him who has all the power in his hands—just as I used to think it was my duty to speak freely, since through me freedom still lived, now that it is lost I do not think I have any right to say a word against his wishes. In the opinion of those philosophers who alone grasp the true meaning of Virtue, the wise man will prefer nothing to the avoidance of wrong doing." But to Atticus he puts it differently: "As to the letter to Caesar, what view ought I to have taken except what I thought he wanted? What other purpose had my letter save to kow-tow to him? Do you suppose I should have been at a loss for words if I had wanted to tell him what I really thought? But what will the conservatives say? [This in another letter.] That I have been bribed to change my opinions? And what will history be saying of me six hundred years hence? That is a thing I fear much more than the petty gossip of today. Perhaps you will say, 'Hang dignity. It's prehistoric. Look after your own safety.' Oh, why aren't you here! Perhaps I *am* blinded by my passion for high ideals."

When his actions invade the realm of the Moral Duties, on which he wrote a famous treatise, he has the comfortable assurance that Atticus knows the ways of a politician in handling constituents must be judged by some other standard and he never has to bother how to cloak them nicely. His son-in-law, Dolabella, has become politically important, and Cicero writes him a long letter of glowing commendation: "Though I take the greatest pleasure in the glory you have won, I confess the crown of my joy is that in the popular opinion my name is associated with yours. Lucius Caesar said to me, 'My dear Cicero, I congratulate you on the influence you have with Dolabella. He is the first consul since yourself who can really be called a consul.' Why then exhort you and set distinguished examples before you? There is none more distinguished than your own." Cicero sends Atticus a copy of this letter and comments: "What a shameless fellow Dolabella is. He has lost your good graces for the same reason that he has made a bitter enemy of me."

Mark Antony writes to ask a favor and Cicero sends a charming answer: "Your friendly letter makes me feel that I am receiving a favor, not giving one. Of course I grant your request, my dear Antony. I wish you had made it in person. Then you could have seen the affection I have for you." Atticus gets a copy of both letters with the remark: "Antony's request is so unprincipled, so disgraceful and so mischievous, that one almost wishes for Caesar back again."

Occasionally, but very rarely, he mixes his Atticus style with his style of grandeur: "Two of my shops have fallen down. People call it a calamity, but I am not even annoyed. O Socrates, I can never thank you enough. Ye Gods, how insignificant all such things are to me. However, I have got a plan of rebuilding which will make my loss a profit." One can see Atticus first dismayed at the news, next a bit irritated by Socrates, and finally relieved by the profitable plan. Cicero had a way of drawing upon Atticus' resources as if they were his own.

But on the whole one closes the volumes with a sense of disappointment. These intimate letters, written at one of the most interesting moments of history about one of the two nations most interesting to us in all antiquity, are nearly always very dull. They are not history, they are daily life, nonconsecutive, full of trivialities, repetitions. Often they are hardly to be called letters; memoranda, rather, hastily jotted down, the day-book of a busy man. Personal concerns fill them. The great city into which everything in the world, civilized and barbarian, was pouring, becomes Cicero's own little stage monopolized by his own drama. He is too hard-pressed for anything else. Here is a political matter which must be decided at once, or a matter of buying a house, or of choosing a husband for Tulia, or of getting some money for Terentia. Will Atticus write back instantly what he advises. That is the way nine-tenths of the letters are written and it is the reason why he who was not commonplace hardly ever wrote a letter that was anything else. Elevation, power, distinction, were saved up for the orations. He may be writing from Athens (he had lodgings on the Acropolis!), or from Delos, "the marvelous isle," or from strange cities and lonely mountain camps in the unknown east: as far as the

letters are concerned he might as well be in his house on the Palatine. There is never the least sign of interest in his surroundings.
He is in a hurry. The messenger must be despatched and let him
get on to the next piece of work. He is a man of big business.

But through all this mass of unassorted detail a singularly convincing picture emerges of the writer, and in the midst of the tiresome trivialities comes every now and then a comment, a story, a
description, which suddenly stirs to life that far-away dead city.

If only Cicero had not been such a keen politician! The political life over-shadows the social to such a degree that while there
are dozens of letters discussing in deadly detail the chances for
election of this or that long, long ago forgotten candidate, or the
effects of some, ages since, dead and buried measure, only a sentence here and there, at the best a few stray passages, throw a little
light on the way of the world as the smart society of Ciceronian
Rome pursued it.

Luxury is plain to see. Cicero pays nine hundred dollars for
some statues "of Megaric marble," on Atticus' advice, and bids
him also "send the figures of Hermes in Pentelic marble with
bronze heads, which you wrote about, for the gymnasium and
colonnade. I have fallen in love with them. Don't hesitate. My
purse is long enough." What the house with gymnasium and
colonnade must have been like, can be seen in a letter about his
brother's house: "All's right on your estate—nothing left to do
but the baths and a promenade and the aviary. The paved colonnade gives dignity. The columns have been polished and the
handsome curve of the ceiling will make it an excellent summer
room. I will see to the stuccoing. In the bathroom I moved the
stove to the corner of a dressing room because it was so placed that
the steam pipe was directly under the bedrooms. Your landscape
gardener has won my praise; he has enveloped everything in ivy—
even the Greek statues seem advertising it. It's the coolest, green-
est retreat. Statues, wrestling ground, fish pond, water
system—all are fine. Really, an edifice worthy of Caesar—and

there is no more fastidious connoisseur." His brother was in Gaul with Caesar, and it may be assumed Cicero knew he could be depended upon "when I write praising any of my friends, to let them know." The letter ends with one of those touches of nature: "I love your boy, but I am allowing him to leave me, because when he is away from his mother the amount he eats appalls me."

Sometimes we get a glimpse of the vast slave world which did all the work and provided all the amusements. "Do send me two of your library slaves," Cicero writes Atticus, "to help glue pages, and tell them to bring bits of parchment for title-pieces. I say, you *have* bought a fine troupe of gladiators. I hear they fight splendidly. If you had cared to hire them out you would have cleared expenses on those two shows. Enough of that—but, as you love me, remember the library slaves."

Of the shows themselves, the most conspicuous feature of the life as we see it, Cicero speaks only once in detail, an often quoted passage: "The games were of course most magnificent, but they would not have been to your taste. I infer that from my own feelings. Why, they were not as attractive even as games on a moderate scale often are. For what pleasure can there be in the sight of six hundred mules in the *Clytemnestra* or of three thousand bowls in the *Trojan Horse?* Two wild-beast hunts a day for five days— magnificent, of course. But what possible pleasure can it be to a man of culture when a puny human being is mangled by a tremendously powerful beast, or a splendid beast transfixed by a spear? And even if it is a spectacle, you've seen it all often, and there was nothing new that I saw. The last day came the elephants—very impressive, but the crowd took no pleasure in them. Indeed, there was a kind of compassion—a feeling that the huge creatures have some sort of fellowship with humans." Gladiatorial contests Cicero rather inclined to—from moral considerations. People call them cruel, he says, and perhaps they are, as conducted today. But certainly the spectators receive an incomparable training in despising suffering and death.

All through the letters there are allusions to the love the great, luxurious, corrupt and vice-ridden city had for passing prohibitions against luxury, corruption and vice. There is an amusing passage in a letter from a young scoffer Cicero was very fond of, Caelius Rufus, where Cicero is urged to come home to divert himself with the censor's activities: "He's performing prodigies in the matter of pictures and statues. Seems to feel his censorship is to be a kind of soap. Hurry home and join the laugh. Appius busy with pictures and statues!" It was of course delightful. Appius was Clodia's brother and the man who had bribed the consuls.

Only a very mild and limited edition of the *chronique scandaleuse* of the day is to be found. The decorum of the letters is amazing in that day and in that city. There is hardly a suggestion of impropriety even. A sample of his scandal-mongering—there are not above half a dozen in all—is a story he tells Atticus about an unfortunate gentleman who had his baggage searched and among his goods "were found five diminutive busts of Roman ladies—married, all of them! One was Brutus' sister, another, Lepidus' wife. *He* won't fret." This is as far as Cicero will go in the way of an off-color story, and yet he wrote at a time when Rome was full of the vilest vice and the foulest talk. In an age notable for indecency, when Cicero was at his ease and writing just as he felt, he was invariably decent-minded. The scandalous tales passed him by all unheeded. In that respect his letters might have been written by Gladstone to John Bright. "I like modesty in speech," he once wrote. "The Stoics say that nothing is shameful or obscene in the saying of it. Wise men will call a spade a spade. Well, I shall keep as I always have, to Plato's reserves." He goes back to the Greek for his example; all the same, one catches a glimpse of a grave, disciplined restraint which through the centuries had ordered Roman life.

Dinner parties figure largely in the letters. On one occasion Cicero finds himself in very questionable company, "where next me reclined Cytheris [respectable women sat at table]. At such a dinner, say you, was Cicero! Upon my oath, I never dreamed she would be there. However, even when I was young I was never tempted by anything of that sort, much less now that I am old. But I do dearly love a dinner party where I may talk on anything and everything." What he has to eat there is of much less importance; still he never professes to be indifferent to that, either. "I do like high-class food and of a delicate quality," he writes, "but even if you persist in putting me off with the kind of dinner your good mother gives, I won't refuse." The standards of what one ought to have at a party are truly exalted: "Behold my audacity," he tells the same friend. "I have given a dinner to Hirtius without a peacock!"

His own private life figures very little. He divorced his wife when he was sixty and their daughter was old enough to have been married three times, but he never alludes to the divorce or to anything that led up to it. There are many letters to Terentia which are full of affection. "To think that you of all people, noble, faithful, upright, generous, as you are, should have fallen into misery because of me. Nothing is or ever has been dearer to me than you are," he writes her during his exile. "Tullius sends his best love to his wife Terentia and to his sweetest daughter Tullia, the two darlings of his heart." Such a beginning is quite usual in his letters, but gradually the tone grows cool and the last of all is rather a written order than a letter: "I think I shall arrive at my Tusculan villa on the 7th. See that everything is ready. I may have several others with me. If there is no basin for the bath, provide one and all else necessary. Goodbye." Terentia was not a submissive lady, and the divorce followed soon after. A few months later he had married a rich young ward of his and in as many weeks was bitterly regretting his rashness. He tells Atticus: "Publilia writes that her mother is coming to see me and that she will, too, if I will let her. She begs me urgently and humbly to do so and to answer her. You see what a nuisance it is. I answered that I was even worse than when I told her I wanted to be alone and she must not think of coming. I thought if I did not answer she would come; now I don't think she will. But I want you to find out how long I can stay here without being caught." Of course in Rome of easy divorces the marriage was soon ended.

Cicero's reason for wanting to be let alone was that that sweetest daughter of his had just died. He had only two children and his son was never very satisfactory. But Tullia was all that he could desire and he gave her his most devoted love. When she died, about two years before he did, he was utterly desolate. "While she lived," he wrote a friend, "I always had a sanctuary to flee to, a haven of rest. I had one whose sweet converse could help me to drop all the burden of my anxieties and sorrows." For months after, his letters to Atticus show a broken-hearted man. "I don't speak to a soul. In the morning I hide myself in the wood where it is wild and thick and I don't come out till evening. After you I have not a better friend than solitude. I fight against tears as much as I can, but as yet I am not equal to the struggle." It was the deepest personal sorrow of his life.

Through the letters great figures pass perpetually, great still to us today. Mark Antony, "a wretched, insignificant subordinate of Caesar's," Pompey from his height of aloof superiority calls him; "the toy captain," Cicero dubs him jeeringly to Atticus, "who carries round with him that actress Cytheris [the lady of the dinner party?] and in an open litter too. Indeed, they say he had seven litters with him full of his vile creatures, men and women both." Pompey appears often, contradicting on one page what was said on the page before, now the great statesman and superlatively great general who had been the leading man in Rome for years, and then at the crisis of his life when he faced Caesar to see which would rule the world, suddenly showing himself neither a statesman nor a general, as devoid of resolution as of common sense. "His way is to want one thing and say another," that engaging young scamp, Caelius Rufus, writes Cicero, "and yet he's not clever enough to hide what he wants. But," he adds gaily, "he's undergoing a reducing treatment at Bauli and is so extremely hungry, even I am sorry for him."

It will be seen that the letters puncture balloons; magnificence has a way of collapsing. The noblest Roman of them all bears no resemblance whatever to the personage we have watched so often on the stage. Cicero hears that Brutus is to marry Portia, and a good thing, too—the only way to stop the gossip. He goes to Greece and finds that Brutus is insisting that the people of Salamis shall pay him forty-eight percent on the money he has loaned them. "I can't go back on my own edict fixing twelve percent as the rate, even for Brutus," he writes Atticus. "A letter from Brutus"—this shortly after Caesar's assassination. "I enclose a copy. One must confess it's of rather a dubious description—still he does show some sparks of manly courage."

Brutus' mother at any rate was not deficient in that respect. One day in his country house, shortly after Caesar's death, Cicero is present at a meeting of three great ladies, Servilia, Tertulla and Portia, Brutus' mother, sister and wife. They talk over the situation: both Brutus and Cassius have been insulted by receiving from the senate appointments to insignificant offices, Cassius' being merely to buy corn in Sicily. As they deliberate, "in came Cassius with flashing eyes and declared he would not go to Sicily." Whereupon Servilia promised she would take the matter in hand herself: "Servilia says she will cut the corn supply business out of the senatorial decree." It is a curious little picture of those elusive persons, the Roman women. Obviously, Servilia knew that she had the senate in her pocket.

The great Augustus, first Emperor of Rome, the autocrat whose word was final throughout the civilized world, appears a very human young man before the splendid trappings of royalty covered him up. Cicero shakes his head over him many a time. "It's a grave question how far one can trust one of his age and bringing up," he writes a few months after Caesar's death. "His father-in-law whom I saw at Astura thinks he is not to be trusted at all." "He's such a boy," this in a letter dated a year before Augustus handed Cicero over to Antony to be murdered. "He thinks he can call the Senate right away. Who will come? Yet the country towns are enthusiastic about the lad. Crowds to meet him and cheer him. Would you ever have believed it?" "A praiseworthy youth who had better be rewarded—and removed," is his final pronouncement. That remark was repeated to Augustus; three months later he agreed to Cicero's assassination.

Cleopatra, unfortunately, enters rarely and only once at any length. To Cicero she was not precisely the queen

> Whom everything becomes, to chide, to laugh,
> To weep—

"Cleopatra. How I detest the woman. You know she lived just across the river from me for several months. Anything more insolent—." Clearly a royal snub had been administered. Something on Cicero's part royalty had deemed presumptuous. It is a pity the interview has been lost. Cicero was not the man to submit in silence. A consular of Rome and a petty barbarian potentate would have been his evaluation of the opposing forces.

So at the touch of the letters, magnificence even in the most magnificent vanishes. The stately personages great tragedy has made live for us upon exalted heights, through these day-by-day records come down to the same levels where we live ourselves. Yet it is true that every one of them, Pompey, the solemnly inefficient, Brutus, the usurer, Portia, the indiscreet, Antony, the waster, even the insolent queen, were able to rise to greatness on occasion. If they could not maintain it during their lives they could reach it in the way they died, perhaps a matter of hardly less importance.

VI

Caesar and Cicero

Caesar, the greatest man Rome produced, as we all believe with perhaps no very definite notion why, is seen less distinctly than any of the other notable personages Cicero discusses with his friends. That is our great loss, for Caesar was not given to explaining himself. A book, no matter on what subject, could hardly be less personal than his *Gallic War*. It is the one example in literature of an impersonal autobiography. Caesar figures on nearly every page, but in exactly the same way as all the other characters do. In a narrative which shows him overcoming incredible obstacles, facing almost insuperable odds, carrying overwhelming responsibilities, in perpetual danger of defeat and death—through all the account of what must have filled him with joy and grief and despair and triumph, there are only two exceptions to the perfect detachment of the record, only two passages, both very brief, in which there is a trace of personal feeling.

The first is merely a sentence, at the end of the account of his first campaign: "The Senate, informed of these successes by Caesar's letters, decreed a thanksgiving of fifteen days, a number never allowed to any general before." The statement is almost naïve enough to be Cicero's. A little ray of light shoots from it into that inscrutable thing, Caesar's heart. He was proud of that thanksgiving; he loved being more honored than any man before. With the words he comes down for a moment from the unhuman heights on which he sets himself.

In the second passage, which belongs to the narrative of the

war, the emotion is unmistakable. Once a man he loved was sent
by him into what proved to be the extremest peril, and Caesar suf
fered so much, the story bears the impress. "A young man," he
describes him, "of great merit and politeness and of a singular
integrity," was despatched as envoy to the German camp, where
he was seized and held. For all Caesar knew, they killed him. He
attacked and routed them, and then "the young man, bound with
a triple chain, dragged along by his keepers in their flight, fell in
with Caesar himself as he pursued the Germans. Nor was the victory itself more grateful to the general than his good fortune in
rescuing his intimate and familiar friend and to have the success
of the day no way diminished by the loss of one he esteemed so
highly."

With the words, the polite and meritorious young man vanishes from history, and in all the rest of Caesar's writings, the
seven books of the *Gallic War* and the three of the *Civil War* (often
judged not his) there is nothing comparable to his story. Even the
annihilation of a legion and the rescue of another just on the point
of annihilation are recounted with no more feeling than if the nar-
rator were a historian of deeds done centuries before him.

It is not to be supposed that he followed a deliberate plan to
leave himself out. He had one thing alone in his mind, his campaigns, and he thought of himself only as he was concerned in
them. Certainly he wrote without an idea that he would ever have
a reader who would think of anything else. He was always a man
of few words; about himself he did not talk at all. A result of this
reticence was that legend became extremely busy with him;
indeed, it took possession of him not long after his death when his
first biographer gratified a curious world. For years he was the
most talked-of man in Rome and the stories, of course, grew
always bigger and usually blacker. It is the greater pity that Cicero, who knew him from boyhood and was the one man among
his contemporaries with ability enough to understand him,
should mention him only briefly and rarely. No clear picture of

him can be drawn from the letters. The truth is that Cicero did
not try to see him clearly and was always shifting his point of
view. But not his feelings; they remained the same: he never liked
him. That is as plain to see as is Caesar's liking for him. Up to the
crossing of the Rubicon the letters mention Caesar's name oftenest because of some service he has done or wishes to do Cicero.
Caesar wanted his friendship and Cicero never gave it to him.

And yet Cicero was a good friend. Perhaps more than any other
quality, the letters show his warmth of heart and the many people
he was able to spend it upon. Expressions of devoted affection are
common. He writes a man for whom he had got a post abroad:
"'How hard to please are those who love'—at first I was annoyed
that you did not like being where you are; and now it gives me a
pang of pain when you write that you do. I am distressed that you
can find pleasure without me!" He is laughing at himself, but
even so the words ring true and others like them are found again
and again. "All men believe," he wrote elsewhere, "that life without friendship is no life at all."

No doubt these friends were often among the powerful; nevertheless some of the very warmest and sweetest of the letters are
written to the slave who was his secretary. He was not strong, and
Cicero showed a constant and tender anxiety for him: "Let your
health be your only care; leave everything else to my care. Manifest as much regard for yourself as you do for me. Add this to the
numberless services you have done and I shall value it more than
them all. Take care, take care of yourself, Tiro mine." There are
many such little notes to this beloved servant.

But what was given to a slave in full measure Caesar never won
for himself, although year after year he tried. To be sure, away
back in 63 (B.C., N.B.) he had voted against putting Catiline's fel-
low-conspirators to death, than which he could have done nothing worse in Cicero's eyes. All the same, when three years later he
formed the coalition with Pompey and Crassus he invited Cicero
to join, as great a proof of his esteem as he could have given. Cic-

ero refused, why, can only be conjectured; the letters do not mention the offer nor indeed the coalition, except for a single reference to "three unbridled men." He refused, too, Caesar's next friendly move made soon after, when he had been given an office as notable in its results as any that has ever been given, the governorship of "Cisalpine Gaul and the Provinces beyond the Alps." He asked Cicero to go with him. Atticus is told, "Caesar most liberally invites me to take a place on his personal staff."

Back of that offer was the hero of the Good Goddess festival, young Clodius, although no one would have been more surprised than he to know it. He was easily the most popular man in Rome at the moment and as dangerous an enemy as one could have. It might be supposed that he was Caesar's enemy, too, but not at all. The scandal and the divorce and Pompeia's disgrace had somehow all been wiped off the slate, to Caesar's lasting shame, Plutarch says, but political expediency is always abominable in Plutarch's eyes. Clodius was to defend Caesar's interests during his absence. Caesar knew he was planning a spectacular vengeance on Cicero, and the invitation was given to get him away where he would be safe, and also, perhaps, where he would be harmless. After he refused to join the coalition, Caesar's idea of him was always that as a politician he was a liability. But life outside Rome was desolation to him and Caesar's company certainly nothing by way of compensation. He would not go, and soon after, Clodius triumphantly passed the law which cut him completely off from his beloved city and sent him into exile, the most forlorn, homesick wanderer that ever there was.

Pompey, who, Cicero writes Atticus, "swears he will not see me injured [by Clodius] if it costs him his life," acted as was his way at a crisis, held grandly aloof and would take no part at all. When Cicero went to beseech his help and even flung himself at his feet, he answered coldly that he could not interfere, and he did not so much as stretch out his hand to raise the stricken man. Unforgivable, one would suppose, from a friend, and Pompey was an old friend; and yet when after more than a year of misery in foreign parts Cicero was recalled with Pompey's approval, he not only forgave him, he felt himself ever after deep in his debt. Inexplicably—nothing in the record gives any reason why—the plaster god which Pompey throughout the letters appears to be, all gilding outside and inside all hollow, had Cicero's unspeakable devotion. Years later when the war had begun for the leadership of the Roman world and Pompey fled before Caesar, abandoning Italy to him, Cicero could write: "The one thing that tortures me is that I did not follow Pompey when he was rushing to ruin. Since then I have never approved his course and he has never ceased to commit one blunder after another. And never a letter to me. But yet, now my old love breaks forth; now I miss him intolerably. Day and night I gaze at the sea and long to take flight to him."

With Caesar it was just the other way about. Cicero would not like him, no matter what he did. Caesar sent him many letters during the years he was in Gaul; he succeeded at least in convincing him that he could count upon him. All of the letters have been lost, but one of them Cicero quotes from in his answer: "A letter has just come from you saying, 'As to the man you have recommended to me, I will e'en make him king of Gaul. Send me somebody else to give a post to!'" It is delightfully said. The words, so few, are like a tiny snapshot—no pose; for the moment the great general has gone: a laughing face looks out and there is something warm beneath the gaiety. He wrote Cicero, so the latter tells his brother, "a most beautiful letter," when his dearly loved daughter died, the young Julia, Pompey's wife, who as long as she lived kept peace between the two men who both adored her.

Even on his arduous campaigns he took the trouble to write often. "A most cordial letter from Caesar," Cicero writes Atticus. "The result of the war in Britain is looked forward to with anxiety. There is not a scrap of silver on the island, no booty either except slaves—and I don't fancy there will be any with literary or musical talent among *them*." And again, some three weeks later: "On

October 24th I had a letter from Caesar in Britain, dated September 25th. Britain is settled, hostages taken. No booty, but a tribute imposed, [it was never paid], and they are bringing back the army."

That was in the year 54. Then for several years Caesar drops out of the letters except now and then in those Caelius Rufus writes Cicero in Cilicia: "Lots of talk about Caesar—not so very nice. One fellow says he's lost his cavalry, which I don't doubt; another that he's hemmed in among the Bellovaci, cut off from the rest of the army. All secrets these. Domitius puts his finger to his lips before he even begins to speak."

The date of that letter is 50, the year when, frightened by Caesar's triumphs in the west and his increasing popularity in Rome, the senate and Pompey lightly determined to put him down. Caelius writes: "Pompey is resolved not to allow Caesar to be consul unless he hands over his army; Caesar is convinced there is no safety for him without the army; he wants to compromise—have both give up their armies." This fair proposal was rejected. Rome had no idea yet what Caesar was like. "When Pompey was asked," Caelius continues, "'What if Caesar is minded to be consul and keep his army too?' he replied with the utmost suavity, 'What if my son is minded to lay his stick across my shoulders?'" "Pompey has a perfect contempt for Caesar," Cicero writes Atticus. The result of this attitude was that Caesar crossed the Rubicon early in the next year and the fight was on, to end eighteen months later in Pompey's defeat and death.

Almost at once Caelius Rufus, the gay adventurer, and Atticus, the far-seeing and prudent, go over to Caesar, significant straws, both of them. Caelius flings himself into the cause with enthusiasm. "Did you ever see a sillier fellow than your Pompey," he writes Cicero from Caesar's quarters in northern Italy, "stirring up all this mud with his feeble inefficiency? And did you ever read or hear of anyone keener in action than our Caesar or more moderate in victory?" Of Atticus' right-about-face we know only

from a letter Cicero writes him: "When men like you and Pedu-
caeus are going to meet him [Caesar] at the fifth milestone, surely
his belief that he is right will be strengthened. 'What harm in
that?' you ask. None—but yet the outward signs of the distinction between true feeling and pretense are all upset." Poor Cicero.
Atticus is merely acting according to the principles of expediency
that he and Cicero had always acknowledged to each other they
followed, but when it comes to the point of deserting Pompey and
the senate just because they are not succeeding, Cicero cannot do
it and it is bitter to him that Atticus can. And yet a few months
earlier he had written him: "What am I to do? I know if it comes
to fighting it would be better to be beaten with Pompey than
conquer with Caesar. But consider by what trick I can keep Caesar's good will."

From then on until Pompey's defeat there is nothing in the letters Cicero himself writes that helps to explain Caesar. He is only
denunciatory. Caesar is "that viper we have cherished in our
bosom"; "the prince of scoundrels"; a "wretched madman" who
has "never seen the shadow of honor and right." But there are two
letters of Caesar's included in the correspondence which are
remarkable documents. During Cicero's long and agonizing
struggle to follow what he felt was the path of honor and take his
stand with Pompey and the losing cause, Caesar never ceased beg-
ging him—not to join him, that, it is clear, he instantly saw Cicero would not do—but not to join Pompey either. He writes
him—the letter is inscribed *On the march* and the year is 49—
"You will have done a serious injury to our friendship and con-
sulted your own interest very little if you show that you have
condemned anything that I have done, the greatest harm you
could do me. By the right of our friendship, I beg you, do not take
such a step. What better befits a good and peaceful man and a
good citizen than to keep out of civil dissension? There are some
who approved such a course and were unable to follow it because
of danger." He means himself and the words, so carefully imper-

sonal, are yet one of the few personal expressions of his feelings on record. "But for you," the letter continues, "the evidence of my life, your conviction of my affection, must show you there is no safer or more honorable course than to keep clear of the struggle."

Urgent words, written with strong feeling. It is not to be supposed that politically Cicero was important to Caesar. He had always been a weak and wavering politician. What must have dictated that letter was Caesar's genuine friendship, and also, perhaps no less, his hatred of civil war. He wanted to enlist in the cause of peace the eloquent tongue he had himself often been moved by.

When his letters failed he arranged for a meeting, and Cicero's account of it to Atticus shows how little those two able men, who had known him all his life, understood him. "We were mistaken," so the letter runs, "in thinking he would be easy to manage. I have never seen anyone less easy. After much talk he said, 'Well, come and work for peace.' 'On my own terms?' I asked. 'Am I to dictate to you?' he said. 'Well,' I said, 'I shall oppose your invasion of Spain and I shall mourn for Pompey.' He replied, 'That is not what I want.' 'So I fancied,' said I. 'But that is what I must say if I go to Rome.' So we parted. I am sure he has no liking for me, but I like myself as I have not for a great while. He is very wide-awake and bold—"

Most significant of all is another letter which one of Caesar's officers sent Cicero in an effort to show him Caesar's real aims and so win him over. It is unique in military correspondence. Caesar had written his subordinate: "I made up my mind to act with the greatest moderation and do my best to bring about a reconciliation with Pompey. Let us see if in this way we can win all hearts and secure a lasting victory. It is a new way of conquering, to use compassion and generosity as our defenses. I captured one of Pompey's officers. Of course I acted according to this plan of mine and set him free at once."

There was nothing weak and wavering in Caesar. He kept to his plan; he followed this new way of conquering. When Pompey

was defeated, one after another of the men who had supported
him were given a free pardon. There has never been a victor more
merciful. In that pitiless ancient world he stands alone. Cicero,
eagerly forgiven and welcomed back to Italy, was won to an apparent admiration. He writes one and another of his friends, "We
find him daily more yielding and conciliatory"; "He has a mild
and merciful nature"; "I continue to enjoy his extreme kindness
to me." And on one occasion when Caesar pardons a man who had
not only opposed him but deeply insulted him, Cicero even has a
moment of enthusiasm: "It seemed to me so glorious a day that I
imagined I saw before me some fair vision of the Republic rising
from the dead."

Such expressions, however, are all in letters to other people,
never to Atticus. The only praise he ever gave Caesar in the letters
where he spoke the truth was praise of his writing: "I forgot to
enclose a copy of my letter to Caesar—not, as you suspect, because
I was ashamed of seeming a flatterer. I have a high opinion of
those books of his, so that I wrote without flattery, and yet I think
he will read it with pleasure." For the rest, the allusions are brief
and cautious: "I give you a free hand. Only take care that nothing
is done to offend the great man." Atticus would not have welcomed just then any denunciations of the great man, nor would
Cicero have dreamed of writing them. He was doing everything
in his power to stand well with Caesar, and postal messengers did
not always carry mail to the right person.

The last glimpse of Caesar is in a letter dated about six months
later and less than three months before the Ides of March. Cicero
gives him a dinner party, a very splendid affair. "It passed off perfectly delightfully," he tells Atticus. "A formidable guest, but he
left no regret behind. Until one o'clock he admitted no one: at his
accounts, I believe. Then he took a walk, and after two, his bath,
and then, when he had been anointed sat down to dinner. He was
undergoing a course of emetics so he ate and drank as he
pleased—a lordly dinner and well served,

Well cooked, well seasoned and the truth to tell,
With pleasant discourse all went very well.

We were all friends together. Still he isn't the sort of guest to whom one would say, 'be sure to look me up on your way back.' Once is enough. There was no serious talk but plenty of literary—" a sentence typically Roman in its evaluation of what was really worth men's sober attention.

In Cicero's next letter Caesar is dead. The conspirators did not ask Cicero to join them, to his never-ending regret, he protests in several letters. There were no bounds to his enthusiasm at first: "Though all the world conspire against us, the Ides of March console me. Our heroes accomplished most gloriously and magnificently all they could." So for the next two months. Then there is a change. He begins to distrust Brutus and Cassius as leaders. They will not take any decisive steps. They keep away from Rome and do nothing. "The deed was done with the courage of men, but with the blind policy of a child," he writes Atticus in May. And when he goes to see them a month later he finds "a ship breaking up or rather in wreckage. No plan, no reason, no system." Then for a moment he remembers the friend who had stood by him through just such a shipwreck: "For Caesar, somehow, was most patient with me." But that touch of regret and wonder stands quite alone. His final words are as sweeping a condemnation as has ever been spoken of one man by another. In the treatise on moral duties, written in the year of Caesar's death and the year before his own, he says: "So great was his passion for wrongdoing that the very doing of wrong was a joy to him for its own sake." This is Cicero's obituary over Caesar.

It is not possible to explain his feeling as due merely or mainly to his devotion to the Republic and consequent hatred of the man who took the supreme power himself. To the end of his life he loved and praised and mourned Pompey, but long before he joined his camp in Greece he had seen clearly that he was fighting for one thing only, his own domination. "Absolute power is what Pompey and Caesar both have sought," he wrote Atticus. "Both want to be kings." "Pompey's idea from the first has been to bring savage tribes to ravage Italy." Nevertheless, his affection for him never failed. Something else was responsible for his steady dislike of Caesar. Alone among his contemporaries he was qualified to understand him, and no doubt Caesar felt this. His powerful and brilliant mind could find a companionship in Cicero no one else could give him. Except for him he was surrounded by petty minds, mean and limited spirits. But Cicero would have none of him, and so far as is known, except for Mark Antony, Caesar never had a close and steadfast friend. The two officers he most trusted turned against him; Brutus whom he loved killed him, and no other men are mentioned as being on terms of intimacy with him.

The devotion of his soldiers to him, affirmed in many stories, must be a fact. He could not have done what he did without it. The speech in which it is always said he quelled a mutiny with a single word, calling his men not fellow-soldiers as was his custom, but citizens, civilians, shows a great deal more about his methods than the mere clever use of a term.

It was a most critical moment for him. He was in Rome after Pompey's defeat, on the point of sailing for Africa, to put down the powerful senatorial army there. In the city he was surrounded by bitter enemies. His whole dependence was his army, and the best and most trusted legion in it mutinied. They nearly killed their officer; they marched to Rome and claimed their discharge; they would serve Caesar no longer. He sent for them, telling them to bring their swords with them, a direction perfectly characteristic of him. Everything told of him shows his unconcern about danger to himself. Face to face with them, he asked them to state their case and listened while they told him all they had done and suffered and been poorly rewarded for, and demanded to be discharged. His speech in answer was also characteristic, very gentle, very brief, exactly to the point:

"You say well, citizens. You have worked hard—you have suffered much. You desire your discharge. You have it. I discharge
you all. You shall have your recompense. It shall never be said of
me that I made use of you when I was in danger, and was ungrate-
ful to you when danger was past."

That was all, yet the legionaries listening were completely
broken to his will. They cried out that they would never leave
him; they implored him to forgive them, to receive them again as
his soldiers. Back of the words was his personality, and although
that can never be recaptured, something of it yet comes through
the brief, bald sentences: the strength that faced tranquilly deser-
tion at a moment of great need; the pride that would not utter a
word of appeal or reproach; the mild tolerance of one who knew
men and counted upon nothing from them.

One more speech famous in antiquity is reported which shows
the same characteristics. It was made to his officers during the war
in Africa. The senatorial forces there had formed an alliance with
a barbarian king of whom frightful stories were told. Caesar heard
that his centurions were nervous at the report of the king's
approach with an overwhelming army, and he called them
together. "You are to understand," he said, "that within a day
King Juba will be here. He has ten legions" (their own force was
very inferior), "thirty thousand horse, one hundred thousand skir-
mishers, three hundred elephants. Your part is neither to think
about the situation nor to ask questions. I tell you the truth and
you must prepare for it. If any of you are frightened I will provide
you with means for going home."

"I am told," Cicero said to him in a speech made in the senate
a few weeks before his assassination, "that you often say you do
not wish for longer life. I have myself with sorrow heard you say
that you have lived long enough." The night before the Ides of
March, a chronicler relates, he was at supper with a number of
others when the talk turned on what was the best kind of death.
Caesar, who was signing papers while the rest argued, looked up

and said: "A sudden one." The story, of course, is too apposite, but the man who first told it understood character. It is just what Caesar would have said.

Two other accounts of him by contemporaries have come down. Sallust, who wrote a history of Catiline's conspiracy, describes Caesar at some length, but dwells only upon his kindness and leniency. He was always "giving, relieving, pardoning, a refuge for the unfortunate"; "He was marked out by his humanity and benevolence"; "He cared for his friends' interests and neglected his own." It is undoubtedly the report of a partisan; Sallust was an officer of Caesar's and Caesar thought highly of him, but it agrees in general with Cicero's account—who was no partisan. The speech Caesar made against putting the conspirators to death, Sallust gives in full, and all the probabilities are that it is essentially accurate. Certainly Sallust was not present when it was spoken, but there were short-hand writers in Rome, and the occasion was a great and notable one. Furthermore, those who had heard the speech would be Sallust's readers and the very ones whose approval would mean most. It is not credible that he wrote what the senate would know was false. The speech is brief and calm, a closely reasoned, unemotional appeal to abide by the law. Laws are made to be men's defenses not only against others but against their own selves. They are man's safeguards against man's passions. The proposal before the house is to put citizens to death. It is illegal. Whenever in the past the great bulwark of the law has been weakened, the consequences have invariably been calamitous. If by any act now it should be seriously impaired, the danger is that it may be ultimately completely overthrown, to the disaster of all within the state.

But what could this impersonal rationality mean to furious, frightened men whose ears still rang with Cicero's impassioned appeals to everything mortal and immortal except the rational? Cicero is an authority for Caesar's brilliant promise at the bar when in his youth he began a career as a lawyer. None of his speeches there have survived and all that can be said is that he must then have changed his style completely in his later years. Cicero was the model for the Roman bar; his powers of terrific invective, of playing upon people's emotions, of firing them to anger or melting them to tears, of making the eagle scream—the bronze Roman eagle—with appeals to republican glory and ancestral purity of hearth and home—this overpowering onrush of eloquent language would surely never have found a rival in the direct, terse, simple words which are all that Caesar has left behind him.

There is still another portrait of Caesar drawn by a contemporary. In those last years of the Republic a fierce young poet was walking the streets of Rome and noting with passionate scorn in bitter, jeering verses the corruption he met with there. It would be hard to find in all the range of literature anything more different from Cicero's letters than Catullus' poems. To pass from one to the other is rather like passing from Archdeacon Grantley and the pleasant people of Barset to Swift at his most violent. Cicero by birth and by nature is the decent, comfortable bourgeois always; Catullus, the aristocrat by temperament turned rebel against the world and everything decent and comfortable in it.

The first of the two poems in which he expresses his opinion of Caesar turns on one Mamurra, of whom Cicero wrote to Atticus: "Do I approve of Caesar's military power being extended? If I did I would approve of the throwing away of the Campanian lands, of my own banishment, of the wealth of Mamurra—" Catullus thought the same about that wealth: "Who can witness, who endure, this thing? Only he who is himself without shame, greedy, a swindling gamester. Mamurra have the wealth of Gaul beyond the Alps and farthest Britain? O Rome, decadent in your debauchery, will you witness these things and endure? Now, arrogant, money rolling off him, he goes to every bed of all alike. Was it for this, O general, great as never another, that you went to that farthest island of the west? You foster this thing of evil? Is it for this, O Caesar, Pompey, that you have brought ruin upon all."

The second poem leaves nothing further to be said in the way of personal malediction: "How prettily they agree, Mamurra, Caesar, each as vile as the other with the vice of decadents. No wonder either. The dirt that fouls both has sunk deep in, nor will be washed away. Sick alike, in the same bed, sweet twins, elegantly learned in adultery, both, and one as greedy for it as the other—how prettily they agree."

Did that loud furious voice, shouting out filth of vilest abuse, not reach Cicero's ears when Caesar seemed to him, too, all that was most hateful? He never mentions Catullus; he never hints at any sort of vice in Caesar. With all their decent propriety, the letters give a clear enough picture of Mark Antony's habits. It would seem natural to find in them some allusion of the kind to Caesar's if they had been as Catullus made out. But Cicero is completely silent. Once in a speech he remarked that there was no young man in Rome with any attraction against whom such things had not been said.

The century after Caesar's death heard other tales about him that bore out Catullus' accusation, as well as endless stories of ladies who loved him, but they are not for the chronicler to pass on. There is no contemporary evidence in the case except Catullus, and a complete absence of the judicial quality seems to have distinguished that passionate young man beyond all else. It will be with Caesar as with other men accused of infamies which cannot be proved or disproved, people will believe or not according to their own temperament.

As his contemporaries saw him he was a contradiction, and so he remains. Plutarch quotes a description of him from Cicero which makes credible the many accounts that he was excessively dandified, always an elegant. "When I see his hair so carefully arranged and observe him adjusting it with one finger, I cannot imagine it should enter such a man's thoughts to subvert the Roman State." Yet all reports agree that he could fight—and swim—with the best of his soldiers, and that he not only endured exceptional hardships easily, but practiced always a notable temperance in food and drink. If he was really sick with the diseases of the sewer his vigor was truly astounding. He was—probably—nearing fifty-eight when he died. During the three years preceding he had carried on successful wars in Greece, Egypt, Asia Minor, Africa, Spain, in the accounts of which occur constant references to his outstanding characteristic, swiftness—of mind, in anticipating the enemy's next move, of body, in always arriving long before it seemed possible.

He was reported as fearfully cruel in Gaul and notably merciful in Italy. As regards the first, he is the chief witness against himself. Four times he tells of terrible severity, of whole tribes of Gauls or Germans wiped out or sold into slavery. Each time the people in question had broken an agreement—or Caesar thought so—and he was fighting in a hostile country with no possibility of help from anywhere. In all other cases he makes himself out a lenient conqueror, and the fact that during the long struggle with the Pompeians there was no rising in Gaul against his rule speaks for his wisdom in exercising it.

Before he left Rome for the west the splendor of the gladiatorial games he held had outdone all others and were always spoken of as a cause of his popularity with the lower classes, and yet a curious little story of him has come down in a life of Augustus: "As often as Augustus attended the gladiatorial games, he would take special pains to appear absorbed by the spectacle, because he wished to avoid the odium incurred by his relative (Caesar) who had been used, when present on such occasions, to turn away and occupy himself with reading or writing."

In the end he remains an enigma except in a single respect, his generalship. Quite possibly that is the way he himself would have had it. At any rate, he cared to put himself before the world only as a soldier. He was too great to be easily pigeonholed. He must be given a place among the men of thought; he was pre-eminent as a statesman and he wrote a book which has held its own for two thousand years. Nevertheless, it is the book of a man interested only in what is outside, in things, which to him included most men and all soldiers. His real place is, of course, with the great captains of the world, who whether they rule over war or industry, act and do not explain.

At the opposite pole stands Cicero. He can be understood through and through. All the hidden things within the heart, the meannesses and weaknesses we least wish seen in ourselves, in his case lie open, completely exposed to strange, critical eyes. His vanity, his hypocrisy, his falsehoods, his cowardice, his dependence upon praise, his love of ease, his terrible difficulty in making up his mind, all these and more he wrote down for the friend he knew would never hold a single one against him, and so he preserved them plain to see forever. It was a hard fate for a man to bring down upon himself who wanted most of all to stand a glorious figure in the halls of history.

"He was without magnificence of mind," Plutarch says in his grave summary of his character. The words are arresting; they bring vividly before us the difference between our scale of values and the Greek and Roman. Magnificence of mind is not among our best-prized virtues today. Caesar had it. When his most trusted officer deserted to the enemy in a time of crisis he sent after him all the possessions he had left behind, horses, slaves, baggage, without a word. After Pompey's defeat they brought him a great mass of correspondence found in Pompey's tent, for him to read and find out who were his enemies in Rome. He burned the whole unread. Behind the action lay fearlessness and self-confidence, both of the essence of magnificence. Cicero had neither. He let Catiline go when he had him under his hand. He denounced him sitting before him in the senate-house; he showed him up to the whole senate as a convicted traitor; he thundered and lightened against him—and allowed him to walk out undisturbed, free to leave the city and put himself at the head of a hostile army. He was consul; a word from him and Catiline would have been in prison, but he was not sure that people were with him, and without that surety he never could act. He had no surety within himself.

Magnificence in a man means one who will live on his own terms, not on those imposed by others. A story which illustrates the point is told by Plutarch. When Caesar was very young, Sulla, the all-powerful, bade him as he had already bidden the obedient Pompey, to divorce his wife and take another of Sulla's choosing. Caesar refused; his property was confiscated; he still refused; a price was put upon his head; he fled and still refused. In the end it was Sulla, the terrible autocrat, who gave in to a boy not yet out of his teens. Cicero lived all his life on terms imposed by others. The matter of chief importance to him was to have approval. To the day of his death this was a source of terrible trouble to him. It made him jealous of everyone else who was approved. Even of Pompey he could write: "The thought that his services to the country might in the dim future be reckoned higher than mine used to prick me to the heart." It was the reason he was forever explaining himself, excusing himself. He could not get on without support, or even without praise.

Plutarch was right, he was never magnificent. But all the same he had virtues to command respect. The negative one of complete personal integrity which Pompey shared with him, and Caesar probably too, is by no means to be lightly regarded. In a city where everything was for sale, to be the exception was admirable. But far beyond that is the fact that whenever it came to a definite choice between what he thought was right and what he knew was safe, he chose the former, at a cost of suffering such as only a man timid and sensitive as he was could feel—such suffering as a man like Caesar never felt. But in spite of the agony it cost him, he held fast to duty when he saw it. "One may do some time-serving," he once wrote, "but when one's hour has come one must not miss it." Nor did he. He joined Pompey when he believed his cause was hopeless and that he was bidding farewell to all that made life worth living.

He was a tired old man, too. He wrote Atticus at the time: "And to speak truth, my life's evening, following peacefully after my long labors, has made me lazy with the thought of home pleasures." All the same he found his way to Pompey's camp across the sea. Lucan's famous line about another faithful adherent of the Republic applies as truly to Cicero in that moment:

Conquering causes are dear to the gods, the conquered to
   Cato.

Once more, when Caesar was dead and there seemed to him a possibility of restoring the Republic, he gave up going to Greece where safety lay, to come back to Rome and fight against the man of the hour, Mark Antony, the greatest power then in Italy, whom he saw as an imminent danger to the state. He died in consequence. He was forced to leave Rome; he went first to one country house, then another. At last he decided to take ship and sail somewhere—anywhere. He was all alone. Not one of the many friends of the letters came forward to stand by him. (The record does not say where Atticus was, but we may feel sure the situation was advantageous.) He embarked, and then—no reason is given—left the boat and returned to the house and lay down upon his bed. He had come to the end of his desire for life. But his servants got him up and into a litter and were hurrying him back to the seashore when Antony's men caught up with them. He told them to set the litter down, and, Plutarch says, continuing to stroke his chin as he was wont to do, he looked steadfastly upon his murderers. Only one man dared strike him; the others stood by, covering their faces. "There is nothing," he once wrote to his son-in-law, "absolutely nothing fairer, more beautiful, more to be loved, than high courage." He had not always been able to show it in his life. In his death he was more fortunate.

VII

Catullus

One holiday morning in the year 57 B.C., the year after Cicero returned from exile, the Roman forum was filled with a gathering unusual to the place. In spite of the festival just beginning, a trial was to be held, and not only the size of the crowd but the fact that many notables were to be seen who would normally never think of coming to court, showed that it was judged an occasion quite out of the ordinary. Ladies of fashion were conspicuous; of all the wits of the town every one had his place there; and not a single young man with any pretensions either to wit or fashion but was well to the fore. There was reason enough for their presence. One of Rome's very great ladies had brought a charge of murder and attempt to poison against one of the most brilliant young elegants in the city. Even more alluring than that, the two had been lately, very lately, closely associated, their names linked together in everyone's mouth. It had really been an acknowledged fact; he had even lived for a time in her house, neither of them being people who would dream of giving up anything they wanted because of what might be said. And now they sat facing each other, accuser and defendant on a capital charge, Clodia, once Cicero's friend, the sister of the hero of the Good Goddess festival and herself the heroine of a thousand scandals, and Cicero's gay and cynical and delightful young correspondent, Caelius Rufus.

Clodia had taken her seat in the front row beside the men who had preferred the accusation for her, not one of them important enough to draw even a passing glance away from her. At this time she had not a shred of reputation left; her name was a byword; yet she sat there as disdainfully superior to the staring, covertly sneering crowd as if she had never strayed an inch from the traditions of the great aristocratic house which had fathered her. Of so much the reader of the record may be sure. The Claudii all had magnificence of a sort: they lived their lives on their own terms and what people thought of them mattered not in the very least. In the crowded forum Clodia saw two persons only, the man who had yielded to her for a brief space, lived in her house, taken her money, and then all in a moment scornfully shaken himself free of her, and the man who was to defend him, the bitter enemy of her and hers, home in triumph from the exile her brother had brought down upon him. No one in Rome but knew Cicero's tongue. Another woman would have stayed safe at home. Clodia took a front seat and faced her foe with eyes that never wavered and a faint smile upon her lips.

One may conjecture that the defendant was less at ease. He was at least ten years younger than the lady and twenty years less experienced. Furthermore, if the verdict went against him, he was ruined, and a life of fairest promise had stretched before him when this terrible accusation loomed up in his path. He might well be thinking that he had acted with reckless folly when he had wearied of an older woman's passion and on the instant flung himself away from her. Care was necessary in dealing with the Claudii. He had not troubled to take any. He had laughed at her advances and gone from her to make the city laugh too. *Quadrantaria* he called her, the lady whose price is a penny, and the taunt went through the town. Whenever Clodia appeared someone would whisper it and everyone catch it up and pass it on. He had scorned her openly, and she had been used only to scorn others herself, to throw carelessly away man after man when they had served her turn. Caelius had been a fool and his only hope to escape paying a terrible price for his folly lay in his advocate.

To Cicero the case was heaven-sent. He had come back to

Rome to find that Clodius had had his beloved house razed to the ground and a temple erected on the site. It was the insult added to injury which seemed hardest of the two to bear. And now was his enemy delivered into his hands. Plutarch says of him that before he started on a speech he was always cold with fright and even when launched into the full current of it could hardly leave off shaking and trembling. It is a credible account. Such high tension and quivering sensitiveness are very often the companions of genius. But, it may well be believed, upon this occasion there was not a trace of either. Cicero was at ease and happy; he was perfectly aware of what he could do.

The case for the prosecution was at an end: Caelius had hired men to assassinate the envoy of the King of Egypt with money Clodia had given him; with this same money also he had bribed slaves to administer poison to her. Witnesses were present to swear to both charges. Cicero rose to answer. He knew the Roman crowd as a master musician his instrument; he could play upon them as skillfully and as surely.

"The whole case, gentlemen of the jury, rests upon Clodia, a woman known not only by her noble birth but by the crowd's complete familiarity with her [laughter]. I wish I need not name her, the more that there has been enmity between me and her husband—I mean, her brother. I am always making that mistake— [a wave of delighted amusement passes over the audience, well aware of the scandal of Clodia's relations with her brother]. And indeed, I never thought to take upon me a quarrel with a woman, especially with one who far from being considered any man's adversary is universally held to be the intimate of all [laughter]. I would not offend her. Let me ask her how she would prefer me to address her—in the grave, old-fashioned style or in the lighter manner of today? If the first, I must summon one to rise from the dead, that grand old blind man, of all her family the most renowned, not sorry today that he cannot see who sits before him. He shall stand here and speak in my stead: Clodia, what have you to do with Caelius? How is it that you were either so intimate with him as to give him money, or so hostile to him as to fear to be poisoned by him? You, your father's daughter, the descendant of generations of men who were Rome's consuls, the wife of a man Rome delighted to honor—why did you seek this intimacy? Was he your husband's friend—was he related to you by blood or by marriage? None of these, O daughter of a house where the women have ever equalled the men in glorious renown. Did I break off a base peace with Rome's bitter foe that you might enter into the alliance of a shameful love? Did I bring water to the city for you to wash away your filthiness? Did I build the great highway that you might take your pleasure on it with strange men?

"But perhaps, Clodia, you prefer me to speak to you as a man of the world? Let me dismiss that stern, rugged figure and choose as my spokesman, most appropriately, that perfect man of the world, your youngest brother, who loves you very much. He asks you what all this to-do is about. Are you out of your head, sister, making such a molehill into a mountain? You took a fancy to the young man next door—to his handsome face and figure. His father gave him little money; you tried to bind him to you with some of yours. But he found he must pay too high for your gifts and he has done with you. What of it? Are there no others? Those gardens of yours by the Tiber which you have fitted up so that all the young men want to take their swim there—what is the use of them if you cannot pick and choose as you want? Why make yourself a nuisance to someone who does not want you?"

The delight of the audience may be imagined, but Cicero has not yet done with Clodia. Caelius he treats indulgently, with a touch of humorous despair over youth's careless pursuit of pleasure. Very sad, no doubt. His client cannot be defended on that score; he did what he ought not. "And yet, gentlemen of the jury, we ourselves can remember the hot youth of some among us today. Understand me, gentlemen, I have no intention of naming anyone, but if I had, you will bear me out, I should have no trouble. To speak plain truth, if any woman throws her house open to whosoever desires, if without disguise she leads a courtesan's life, if she so acts here in the city, in her gardens, at Baiae, that what she is is apparent not only by her gait, her dress, her burning eyes, her freedom of speech, but by such entertainments as only women of that kind offer, would you judge a young man who approached her guilty of wrong or merely bent on a moment's pleasure? Tell me, Clodia, would a man who had intercourse with that sort of woman—completely unlike yourself, of course—[laughter] be disgraced and degraded in your eyes? If you are not such a one, as I grant you, how could Caelius act with you as he is said to have done? If you are, your life makes null and void any testimony from you."

Then he passes on to the charge of poison and his mocking voice takes on the deep sonorous accents of the righteously indignant: "Gentlemen, I saw—I myself saw and with as bitter pain as ever I felt in my life, the excellent Metellus, this lady's husband, dying, him whom the day before I had met in the senate house, enjoying the full strength of his vigorous prime. I saw him struggling to speak, his voice choked with agony, striking the wall in his paroxysms. From that house Clodia comes and dares to speak of the effect of swift poison?" Cicero knew his case was won. No one in the audience but was glad to believe the worst of the woman whose beauty and wealth and arrogance had made bitterly envious enemies for her everywhere. The shrewd lawyer brought his speech to a swift close. It ends with the statement astonishing to the modern reader, that the charge rested on nothing substantial, no logical argument, no conclusion necessitated by the premises, but only on the word of witnesses (everyone there knew they were to be hired for any statement desired, on every street corner) and with a pathetic picture of the poor, wronged, innocent young Caelius and the misery of his noble old father, all due to the vilest of women. The verdict was not so much a vindication of Caelius as an overwhelming condemnation of Clodia. Such was the woman whom life's irony made the heroine of one of the world's great love stories.

It is in the highest degree improbable that Clodia ever realized that she had achieved immortality or that if she had she would have cared. The present was her concern, not the future, to extract from each moment the utmost possible of exciting pleasure. The empty immortality of a name would have meant nothing to her at all. Nevertheless it is hers, not because of her charms or her sins or even her great prosecutor, but only because once she loved for a moment a man who had the power, as few before him or since, to put love's passion into poetry.

This was the young Catullus, the fiery poet who blackened Caesar's name. He came to Rome from Verona, sent by a careful father to be cultivated and polished out of small town ways. He was perhaps twenty or so when he was introduced to the grand house on the Palatine where its brilliant mistress held a salon for all the great world. We must conceive him on his first entrance a very shy young provincial, hesitating on the edge of the gay company. But there is much in his verse to prove that he was extraordinarily attractive and it is impossible not to believe him beautiful, too, with the beauty so strangely given to poets in all ages everywhere. At all events, he drew to himself the attention of the lady of the house and by swift degrees he became her close companion. Clodia was a woman of mind and taste, able to see a distinguished talent. She liked to play the critic and the connoisseur with the gifted young Veronese and they had delightful times tearing bad writers to pieces: "My lady has sworn that if I will make no more bitter, biting verses she will choose out the very worst of all poets and offer up his effusions in a fiery sacrifice. Here they are, the poems of Volusius, so superlatively bad, the gods will have a merry laugh when they see the sacrifice offered them."

This was strong wine for a young head, a country boy preferred to all the elegant worldlings by a most beautiful great lady, full ten years his senior. Of course he fell madly in love and for a time he moved her to love him, perhaps surprised at herself that a youthful rustic could make her feel so much. The story is plain to read in the poems. They have come down to us helter-skelter, in no chronological order; poems that belong to the end of his life are among the first in the collection; but about the order of the love poems there can be no doubt. They speak for themselves.

They are a unique chapter in the literature of love, these "Poems to Lesbia"—it was the fashion for a young man to write to his mistress under an assumed name. Their like cannot be found in all the range of English literature. Only a few poems scattered through the centuries approach them in passion and poignancy. Poets of love there have been many in England, but poets of passion almost none. The truth is that it is nature, not a mistress, who really holds the hearts of English poets, and the lady in the case is apt to be lost sight of amid trees and clouds and birds and, above all, the flowers that grow in English gardens:

> Say Rose, say Daffodil, and Violet blue, with Primrose fair,
> Since ye have seen my nymph's sweet dainty face and ges-
> ture rare,
> Did not (bright Cowslip, blooming Pink) her view (White
> lily) shine
> (Ah, Gillyflower, ah, Daisy!) with a grace like stars divine

The only poems really comparable to those of Catullus are Shakespeare's sonnets and in respect of passion alone. In every other way the two poets are a world apart: Shakespeare torturing language to express not only passion, but the entire universe of man's heart, with death and time and eternity and life's tragedy of joy never fulfilled; and Catullus seeing nothing in the universe but Lesbia and able to speak with perfect simplicity because he felt nothing that was not simple. Never did there hover in his restless thoughts what his pen could not write down. He was Lesbia's most uncomplicated lover whose place was this earth, whose precinct was strictly confined to his own loves and hates. In every way he was limited except one only, intensity. He was a great poet, but he was a Roman, and Romans, however poetically inclined, were not given to thoughts that wander through eternity. There is only one exception in all of Latin literature, Catullus' great contemporary Lucretius, the poet of Greek philosophy.

Catullus could write on other themes, too. He could turn out a charming bit of verse on whatever he pleased, his sailing boat, his little "almost island" home where the lake water laughed in the wind, a dinner party, a friend's grief, or what not. He could honor a marriage with a lovely song and divert himself by telling fairy stories. And he could write any number of diatribes like the one on Caesar and Mamurra, as violent and as coarse as anything found in literature, if indeed they belong to that realm. But a poet is judged by his best; his bad makes no difference whatever in the final estimation of him. Catullus was Clodia's lover-poet and his fame is secure.

His distinguishing characteristic, beyond that of all other poets, is to put love's rapture and agony into words so direct, they seem to leave no veil between the reader and the poet's heart. He pours out what he feels with a burning passion that will have nothing but the plainest expression. Figures of speech, embroidery of lovely phrase and delicate fancy, all the decorations of poetry, are swept aside. When he chose he could use them excellently well. The few long poems he wrote on impersonal subjects he ornamented, often very delightfully, in poetry's usual way, but they are negligible beside the love poems. Only rarely, when an unhappy love is his theme or when, in the midst of most unlikely mythological figures, Lesbia suddenly enters—Catullus cannot keep her out—then the voice is once more his own passionate, ecstatic, anguished voice, speaking in words so fused by his fire, we seem to dispense with them and see only the flame.

The love-story he tells is the concentrated story of all loves. He traverses the whole gamut of lovers' feelings everywhere. But this is not to say that he is the typical lover; such fervor of feeling can never be typical; rather he is the quintessential lover. Into a few brief poems he puts the essence of the passion of love.

The story begins very delicately and exquisitely as young love is wont to begin. Clodia—Lesbia—had a pet bird and the youthful stranger watched her adoringly as she played with it, and one night when he went home he wrote her a poem. No doubt he hesitated long before sending it to her:

> * Sparrow, dearest delight of my sweet lady,
> whom she plays with, who nestle in her bosom,
> Swooping down on her, small, sharp beak all ready,
> when she teases and holds out a swift finger,
> and my radiant lady, my desire,
> answers back with I know not what sweet nonsense,
> solace finds for a moment from her heartache,
> as one sick with a fever feels a respite.
> Would I too could so play with you, sweet sparrow,
> I would lift from my spirit its dark trouble.

Lesbia was pleased with the poem and began to distinguish its author with her notice more and more, and he sent her a second, written in the same strain. But now that dark trouble has been lifted, Catullus is happy; he can make tender fun of his wonderful lady:

* It is not necessary to say that such poems are untranslatable. All poems are. Still, the burning fusion of feeling and expression certainly has its own peculiar difficulties for the translator, and the following translations are offered in the hope of giving the reader an idea not so much of what Catullus' poetry is like, but only of what he himself was like. In each case the original metre of the poem has been reproduced accurately enough to give the reader the feeling of the rhythm.

Gods and goddesses all, of love and beauty,
you too, all who are men of finer feeling,
mourn. A sparrow is dead, my lady's sparrow,
my own lady's delight, her sweetest plaything,
dear to her as her eyes—and dearer even.
Little honey bird, knowing its sweet mistress
Well as ever a girl her own dear mother,
Close to her she would hold him, sweetly nestled.
Where she went he went after, here now, there now,
piping only to her his little bird-note.
Who now goes down the sombre road of shadows,
down where never a one comes back, they tell us.
Ill attend you, O evil gods of darkness.
All things beautiful end in you forever.
You have taken away my pretty sparrow,
Shame upon you. And, pitiful poor sparrow,
it is you that have set my lady weeping,
Dear eyes, heavy with tears and red with sorrow.

When a rival of Lesbia's was praised her poet was quick to attack and defend, and Lesbia laughed delightedly at the verses and, one may be sure, passed them on to others:

Quintia, so says the crowd, is beautiful. I grant her fairness.
Tall she is, too, and erect. So much I give her—no more.
Beautiful? Utterly not. What, beauty where charm is all
      wanting?
Never a spice of salt seasons that heavy flesh.
Lesbia—ah, there is beauty. From top to toe she is lovely.
Venus has lost her grace. Lesbia stole it away.

All of a sudden, it would seem, Lesbia was won. She was a connoisseur of lovers and a poet-lover had not come her way before; she found the combination attractive. Catullus was in heaven:

Live, my Lesbia, love. I live—I love you.
Not a fig will we care what grim old men say.
Setting sun will come back again tomorrow.
We, when once our brief daylight has faded,
needs must sleep an unending night forever.
Give me a thousand kisses—then a hundred.
Now a thousand again—and now a hundred.
Still a hundred—and in one breath a thousand.
And when a thousand thousand we have added,
Stop the count and throw them all together.
So no envious eye bring evil on us,
spying out all the number of our kisses.

But the situation was difficult—how to meet, how to avoid the good Metellus' suspicions—all the troubles that have beset true lovers everywhere. Lesbia of course was experienced in handling a husband under such circumstances:

Lesbia, if her husband is near, speaks ill of me always,
greatest delight thereby giving the blind old fool.
Idiot, not to see she remembers me when she upbraids me.
Silence would prove her heart-whole. Now all her jeers and
    her taunts
show she never forgets. Oh, more than that. Through her
    anger
I see a heart a-flame—she is on fire for me.

But the first trembling, incredible rapture had gone. Catullus was on tenterhooks all the time. Would she come—would she not? When—where—how? He grew irritable from misery:

Lesbia laughs me to scorn all day and never is silent.
But, may I die else, I swear, Lesbia loves me alone.
How can I know? I am like her. I laugh her to scorn all

the day through.
But, may I die else, I swear, Lesbia only I love.

Ecstatic hours came still, but through them, far underneath, there was a fear.

Dearest, my life, my own, you say our love is forever,
What is between us shall be joy of love without end.
Gods almighty, give her the power to promise truly,
speak to me only truth, speak to me from her heart.
So through all our years we shall keep faith, each to the
    other,
bound by a holy bond, lovers eternally.

This poem stands for the culmination of Catullus' love and so of his life that was bound up with his love, and yet already he was learning the agony of doubt. He longed to believe; he could not quite. Into his lines he put the true lover's invariable feeling of the holy purity of a great love, no matter what—a husband in the background or anything else. A passion conceived of as eternally faithful has always been felt to be its own justification and through his life Catullus loved Lesbia only.

But his descent from that high point of—almost—believing that the same holy bond bound her was swift. No doubt the mature woman of the world soon found it trying to be a poet's ideal and something less than passion's lofty heights more agreeable for every day in the year. She wearied of perpetual ecstasies. His agony when he first realized that she was unfaithful to him must be imagined. If he made a poem of it, it has not come down to us. Perhaps it was too terrible for even a poet to be able to write it out. But he was very young and very eager for happiness, and humble, too, with the humility of true love. She was so great, so wonderful—how could he hope she would be his alone? Should he not be content that she, the marvelous lady, loved him best? And he wrote:

So my light, my love, came to me in my arms,
came with Cupid dancing, joyously circling around her,
radiant, shining boy, wrapped in a saffron cloak.
Past are those days. No more can Catullus alone now con-
    tent her.
She goes to others now—only a few—I forgive—
I am no fool like the rest to plague her with jealous com-
    plainings.
For she came not to me by right from the hand of a father,
here to my house—these rooms, sweet with Assyrian
        scents,
but through the secret night to give me love's wonderful
        bounty,
gifts that she stole away, robbed from a husband's heart.
Therefore this is enough, if only when I—I—am with her,
that day a white stone marks, shining bright in her heart.

Lesbia, however, was used to varied entertainment. She never
had an idea of confining herself to "only a few," and Catullus' for-
giveness mattered less and less to her. From then on he was living
in the specially fiery hell reserved for great passions wronged. In
his first agony he wrote two lines which express within their brief
compass what that experience is like:

I hate and I love. Why—how—can it be, perhaps you will
    ask me.
That I know not. What I feel, that I do know. I am tortured.

He knew her now, and her sweet words meant nothing any
more:

Ah, what a woman says in the arms of a lover who wants her,
Write on the wings of the wind, give to the rushing stream.

He knew everything, but he could not free himself:

> Lesbia, once you would say none knew you, only Catullus,
> nor would you choose in my stead even a god—Jove him-
>   self.
> Then I loved you not as the common herd loves a mistress,
> but as a father his son—so you were dear to me.
> Now I know you indeed. The flame that is in me burns
>   fiercer,
> yet I see you clear, small and shallow and cheap.
> What? You cannot understand? The wrongs you do to
>   your lover
> force him to love you more, but, ah my dear, prize you less.

He had come far from that young fresh world of enchantment where he watched the sparrow play. He was only in his early twenties, but he would never enter it again:

> Yours is the guilt, my Lesbia, to this pass you have brought
>   me, where love's duty works ruin to love itself.
> So that I have no power to wish you were best among
>   women,
> Yet no power to cease loving you through all you do.

She had certainly been trying to hold him in spite of all this anguish of bitterness, but a day came when she did not try any more. She had done with him and in his passion-torn, despairing young heart he found courage to face the truth:

> Poor wretch Catullus, end this frantic folly now,
> and what you see is dead give up for lost, poor fool.
> A time was once when golden suns shone bright for you,
> when you went only where a girl was pleased to go,
> a girl more loved than any will be loved again.

Then there was merry sport for two, unstinted joys,
what you would have and what your lady, too, liked well.
Then golden suns in very truth shone bright for you.
She wants no more. Then do not you, infirm of will.
When she would flee, will you run after—live a wretch?
Now force your heart—now steel your stubborn will—be
    hard.
Goodbye, my girl, Catullus has made hard his heart.
No more pursuit—to cold reluctance no more prayers.
It is you will suffer pain when no one prays to you.
Oh, you are evil. Yet what life awaits you now—
Who now will go to you? To whom will you seem fair?
Whom will you love now—swear that you are his alone?
Whom kiss and kissing keenly, hotly, bite his lips?
But you, Catullus, come, an end. Make hard your heart.

His dearly loved brother had lately died in the distant east; his grief for him, his old father who needed him, his sick longing for change, called him home from the city of his suffering and he went back to Verona. There he found money troubles, and as the quickest way to be free of them, he got a post with a new governor on the point of leaving for his province, and he went to the east in his train. He made no money, the province having been already drained dry by Roman fortune hunters, but one great wish he did fulfill, he went to his brother's grave and he wrote a poem, ranked among his best, which shows the tenderness there was in him.

Over many lands and many seas I have travelled,
only to stand by a tomb, brother, to weep what is lost.
Give you death's last gift, tears, words of sorrowful part-
    ing,
tears to the careless earth, words to the silent dead.
But since fate has taken you, you, your very self, from me,
brother, pitied, beloved, gone from me in your youth,

these rites now I pay, from olden time taught our fathers,
weeping pay to the dead what to the dead is due.
Wet with a brother's tears, receive from my hand the last
     tribute.
And forever, my dear, greeting—forever goodbye.

But his love story was not yet ended. Lesbia called him back.
Probably he went to Rome of himself, moved in part by the terrible need to see her. And then—did she meet him one day in a
crowd, see him avoid her with visible hatred and scorn, and suddenly feel an amused determination to show him her power—
show herself, too, perhaps, for she was nearing forty and needed
reassurance. So she lifted a white hand and beckoned to him and
he fell at her feet:

When, past hope, there comes to the starving heart its
     desire,
comes after long despair, that—that—is the heart's best
     joy.
So joy best of best and richer than wealth has come to me,
     given to my desire, Lesbia, you yourself.
Back to my hopeless desire you came, you gave yourself to
     me,
Oh, a day of light, marked with splendor for me.
Where is the man who lives more blessed than I am—I
     only?
Who could ask of gods more that life can give?

The reunion could not have lasted long. The house on the
Palatine was changed. The good, stupid Metellus was dead and
strange stories about his death were abroad. People capable of
being shocked visited it no more and they were not missed. It was
a house of excesses; each latest experience must outdo the one
before. What he suffered there Catullus never put into verse.

Caelius Rufus was his close friend. When she took him and brought him into her house to live, Catullus at last saw the end. He broke off, this time for always:

> Hard—it is hard of a sudden to break with a love
>   years-long cherished.
> Yes, it is hard, but you must. This way or that, end it now.
> Here only is your salvation. This fight you must win—
>   here be victor.
>   This you shall do. If you can or if you cannot.
>   You must.
> O Gods, if ever you pity, if ever you bring to the stricken,
>   help in the anguish of death, in life's extremity,
> look on my misery, save him who vows he has lived free
>   from evil.
>   Purge this plague from my blood, make me clean
>   of this taint,
> creeping like slow corruption within me, body, bone,
>   sinew.
>   Not in all my heart space where joy may come.
> No more now I pray she might love me again as I love her,
> not for what cannot be, that she should wish to be true.
> I would be healed, rise up from this torment of sickness
>   that fouls me.
>   O Gods, give only this—this to your worshipper.

He had but a year or two left to live. In his life as in his love he was the quintessential lover, he died young. We hear in his writings of a cough that racked him, the fitting accompaniment to a broken heart. Shortly before his death and after the trial and Clodia's increased recklessness that followed it, he wrote to Caelius:

> Caelius, Lesbia—she, our Lesbia—Oh, that

only Lesbia, whom Catullus only
loved as never himself and all his dearest,
now on highways and byways seeks her lovers,
strips all Rome's noble great-souled sons of their money.

These bitter and poignant words are the last we know of Clodia and her poet.

VIII

Horace

There are people to whom any sense of fitness would assign a short life. Catullus is one of them. Indeed one can hardly conceive of him as living on to old age and the hardest heart could not wish that he had. In his space of thirty odd years he had felt more than most octogenarians, even octogenarian poets. All things were always final with him and moderation in any shape or form impossible. One cannot think without profound weariness of his going on like that. To live perpetually at such an altitude is not for humanity and Catullus would have been worn out long before old age overtook him. Fate at the end was kind to him.

But there are other people whom anyone would like to have live forever, and in that number Horace stands foremost. He would have liked it, too. He had that most delightful gift of enjoying keenly all life's simplest pleasures, a grassy bank by a river, a glowing fire on a cold night, a handful of ripe olives, the sky, the sunshine, the cooling wind. And it is not a doubtful assumption that of those people we would choose out to be immortal nine-tenths would have that very gift. There is none other that helps life along as much, for others as well as for the possessor.

Who would not like to see Horace walk in through his door any day in the year? Immediately everything would seem more agreeable, the cocktails better flavored, the armchairs softer, even the comfort of the warm sheltered room would take on the proportions of an active delight. And the talk would never centre round him-

self. Every attempt to make it do so would be warded off deprecat-
ingly with a touch of gay humor. Sitting in your armchair he
would be the most stimulating of listeners—but any balloon you
launched would be in danger of a puncture from a sly dart of irony,
which yet, with all its cutting edge, would fail to wound.

And if you were in difficulties, if you had spent too freely, or
quarrelled with an important neighbor or offended your employer
or tried to be on with the new love before you were fairly off the
old, you would have in him the most understanding and the
shrewdest, most worldly-wise of advisers.

Horace is the complete man of the world, with tolerance for all
and partisanship for none; able to get on with everyone and at
home everywhere; ready for any pleasure, averse to all the disturbing passions, viewing this earthly scene with some detachment—
and almost never in a state of mind where a laugh comes hard.
The description does not suggest a poet, and indeed no one could
be further from a lunatic or your veritable true lover either than
Horace is. Not a touch of madness in that clear, cool, balanced
head. He is Benjamin Franklin turned poet, or rather, for he never
borders upon the provincial, a poetical Montaigne. He is a poet
whose distinguishing characteristic is common sense, a combination never known before or since.

He was just turned twenty-one when Cicero died and Rome
entered upon one of her worst periods of civil war. He took sides
with Brutus and fought with him through the campaign that
resulted in the final defeat of the republican cause and the establishment of Augustus and Antony as masters of the world. He
came back to Rome heartsick, hardly more than a boy even then,
to find that his little estate had been confiscated and that he was
penniless. A bad beginning, which would have turned many a
man with his great ability and great sensibility into an irreconcil-
able or a misanthrope, and his earliest writing has a bitterness,
even a brutality sometimes, which show how close he had come
to the danger of being permanently warped or stunted. But this

temper of mind soon passed. What Horace did was to face the fact that the Republic was dead and Augustus completely alive, and to get himself a small governmental post as a clerk. He never appeared thereafter in any of his writings as the champion of republican ideas. Quite the contrary. He extolled Augustus to the skies with praise which in any other period except the Roman Empire would have been fulsome almost beyond belief. And yet his reader notes these facts with no sense of condemnation. No one who knows Horace despises him for a time-server. He was not that. He was a man of supreme good sense who saw that the Republic was gone irrevocably and the Empire had arrived to stay, and who chose not to spend his life in a futile effort to turn back the hands of the clock. The result was that he emerged from an experience of early pain and defeat that would have embittered most men, and from a shifting of allegiance that might well have resulted in a cowed and servile spirit, a man of mellow serenity and unshaken independence. These are the triumphs which can be achieved by an evenly poised spirit, by what is one of the rarest of qualities, wisdom.

After dealing him blows so hard and so many, fate turned kind. Augustus' all powerful minister, Maecenas, met him and took a fancy to him, although Horace says of himself he was so shy at the first meeting, he could not get out a sentence without stammering. A great friendship resulted which lasted for thirty years. Maecenas, dying a few weeks before Horace, on his death-bed bade the emperor, "Be mindful of Horatius Flaccus as of myself." Horace's troubles were ended. Maecenas' circle, the best men of the day, was opened to him; Maecenas' purse, too, enough that is for Horace's very simple needs, and he was free. The world was his to do exactly what he pleased.

There was never any question in his mind what that was. In one of his earlier pieces he makes himself go for advice to a famous lawyer, Trebatius, one of Cicero's correspondents: "Direct me, Trebatius. What shall I do? *Trebatius:* Keep still. *Horace:* You mean not write any more verses—not at all? *Trebatius:* That's what I say. *Horace:* I'll be hanged if that wouldn't be best. But I can't sleep all the time—No, it won't do. Everyone has his own way of enjoying himself. Mine is to put words into metre. No use talking about it. Whether peaceful old age awaits me or even now black-pinioned death flies round me, rich, poor, in Rome or, if chance so bids, in exile, whatever my life shall be, bright or dark, I will write."

So he felt through thirty years. All that time he "played with words on paper," as he called his writing, and he never had any other pursuit. Yet the result is only one slender volume. There was one great advantage in the way they did it in Rome, nothing urged quantity upon Horace. The idea could never occur to him that the more pages he filled the better it would be for his purse. In the Roman system the pursuit of literature and the pursuit of money were in large measure separated. In this particular case that was very well for the world, because Horace had by nature, as no one more, the gift of brevity. The result of his freedom to write as he pleased was poetry which belongs to that rare order of verse which is distilled; only the essence left. He gave a good deal of advice, first and last, to would-be writers, and of it all "Be brief" comes first: "So that the thought does not stand in its own way, hindered by words that weigh down the tired ears." And remember always, "More ought to be scratched out than left."

What he taught he practiced, even in his verses which were not poetry, but only prose done metrically. These, his *Satires* and *Epistles* as they are called—he called them *Talks* and *Letters*, better suited to their informality—make up full half of his writing, and they prove beyond all question that what he said of himself was true, he loved "to put words into metre." No other reason can be found for his not having written them in prose. They are little rambling treatises about everything in the world, a great deal of excellent literary criticism and some not so good, a great deal of tiresome copy-book morality and some that is arrestingly true, many wise observations on education, and no less on cooking. He discusses the Epicurean and Stoic philosophies, gives in great detail the mishaps of a journey, makes fun of the way a boring person talks, applies common sense to Greek poetry, and so on and so on, all along the dead level of prose, and saved from being dull only by that admirable brevity. Why he did not use the magnificent medium Cicero had left to Roman literature and write them as little prose essays, would be inexplicable if it were not for his own words.

He loved to produce a smooth-flowing metrical line, and the more complicated the measure the greater his enjoyment. It was a delight to him to try his hand at turning the many varied metres of the Greek lyric poets into Latin, a veritable *tour-de-force*. The first eleven poems of his odes are written in ten different measures, completely unlike each other. His polish and perfection of technique in using these intricate rhythms, his accomplished method, are his alone. No one has ever rivalled him. But the singing gift, the power of "song that wells up as from the bird's throat," which is our idea, more or less, of the lyric poet's endowment, was never Horace's at all. He utterly disclaimed it for himself. Poetical spontaneity, he tells us, was not for him. "Toiling hard" he made his songs.

He was one of the most skilled technicians that ever put pen to paper. Words and phrases were his passion. "Sometimes," he says in discussing composition, "a beautiful word leaps out." So they do continually in his own writing. "A cunning combination can make a familiar word seem brand-new," he writes and he knows well what he is praising. He is the poet of the exquisite phrase, the consummately perfect word. What he says may be negligible, but the way he says it is entrancing. When Hamlet bids Horatio

Absent thee from felicity a while—

there is perfect beauty of poetry in the words, but precisely in those words and no others, in the expression, not the thought. Put that into different words and the poetry has gone: "Refrain from happiness for a time," "Withdraw temporarily from delight"— there is not a particle of significance in either statement. But in

> Men must endure
> Their going hence, even as their coming hither;
> Ripeness is all:

there is something which could not be completely lost, however worded.

A slight alteration would reduce to prose the loveliest phrases in poetry: "In cradle of the rude, imperious surge"; "Through verdurous glooms and winding, mossy ways"; "Under the glassy, cool, translucent wave." But just as Catullus' burning intensity comes through even poor translations, so no verbal change could nullify the passion of

> —for I love you so
> That I in your sweet thoughts would be forgot
> If thinking on me then should make you woe.

"Hitherto shalt thou come, but no further, and here shall thy proud waves be stayed" might be turned into a simple geographical statement, but truth of poetry independent of the particular expression is in, "Though I speak with the tongues of men and of angels, and have not love, I am become as sounding brass, or a tinkling cymbal."

That order of poetry is nowhere in Horace. His thought is hardly more than sagacious at its best and is far oftener commonplace than not. He says of his satires "Change the order of my words and the poetry is gone," and in a sense it is true of everything he wrote. It is never what he says that is important but always how he says it. For this reason he is the most difficult of Latin writers to give an account of to those who do not read Latin.

His poetry is completely untranslatable and all of his admirers
who have tried to turn him into English, very distinguished personages some of them, have only, each in his turn, produced one
more illustration of the fact.

The following examples, perhaps it is necessary to state, are all
translations of the same lines, and, what could certainly not be
deduced without the statement, of lines which rank among the
most famous in Horace.

Addison turned them into:

> The man resolved and steady to his trust,
> Inflexible to ill and obstinately just,
> May the rude rabble's insolence despise,
> Their senseless clamours and tumultuous cries.
> The tyrant's fierceness he beguiles,
> And with superior greatness smiles.

Byron made out of them:

> The man of firm and noble soul
> No factious clamours can control.
> No threat'ning tyrant's darkling brow
> Can swerve him from his just intent.
> Gales to curb the Adriatic main,
> Would awe his fixed, determined mind in vain.

And as Gladstone tried his hand on them, they became:

> The just man in his purpose strong
> No madding crowd can bend to wrong.
> The forceful tyrant's brow and word,
> Rude Auster, fickle Adria's lord,
> His firm-set spirit cannot move,
> Nor the great hand of thund'ring Jove.

Present indications are, therefore, that he will remain a closed book except to the Latinists. What one of his admirers soon after his death called his "curious felicity" can never be transferred to another tongue, and he had no glimpse of new truth to show, no revelation of what lies hidden in men's hearts until the poet speaks it for them.

The idea of the poet as an impassioned, inspired creature, compact of emotion and imagination, must be revised. Horace cannot be fitted into the category. Passion and common sense are not compatible. Passion stands higher—or lower; the two do not operate on the same level. The lover, no matter how averse by nature to follies, is allied to the lunatic for the time being. Horace is a passionless poet always. It is true that his poems are continually decorated with the pretty names of ladies he declares he has succumbed to: Phyllis and Lyce and Cinara, Leuconoe and Pyrrha and Chloe, Glycera and Neaera and Lalage, and many another—of whom some, the number drives one to conclude, had existence only in his verse—but it is more than doubtful whether any woman ever cost him a pang. All the indications are that he was never what we call in love. To our notions a lover, and certainly a poet-lover, must waste, at least a little, in despair and Horace never did, not even a very, very little. He had an exceedingly pleasant time with all of them. His idea of love was that it should add to life's enjoyment and nothing is clearer than that he made it do so. He must have had a wonderful skill in detaching himself from one lovely lady to pass on to another, for there is never a hint at any of the usual accompaniments of such behavior, tears, reproaches, a broken heart or two. In fact they are incredible face to face with Horace. In his presence they would instantly have seemed quite absurd and rather ill-mannered. The anguished maiden would have found herself laughing long before the moment of parting came and she would be left in the end with some excellent advice about her next move. And Horace would lie on a grassy bank by a murmuring river with another fair creature to weave rosy garlands for him and fill his cup with golden wine.

The present writer, warned by the sad results of eminent men's efforts, does not venture to turn into English even a single one of the odes to illustrate this attitude toward the great passion, but a very fair idea of the spirit of Horace's love poetry can be had from the sixteenth century lover-poets of England. Those of the seventeenth century are apt to mingle religion with love, than which nothing could be more foreign to Horace, but those of a hundred years earlier reproduce his attitude and often consciously. He influenced them enormously and the reason was that fundamentally they looked at life and love as he did. To be sure, the comparison holds good only within strict limits. The grace and charm of Horace's verse cannot be matched by the best of them, but they felt about love the way he did and what they produced is far more like him than any translation. He might indeed have written every word of Lyly's *Cupid and my Campaspe played.* Marlowe's *Passionate Shepherd to his Love* is precisely passion as Horace saw it:

> Come live with me and be my Love,
> And we will all the pleasures prove
> That hills and valleys, dales and fields
> Or woods or steepy mountain yields.

Drayton often follows him:

> But see how patient I am grown
> In all this coil about thee;
> Come, nice thing, let my heart alone,
> I cannot live without thee.

Daniel is only Horace's echo when he writes:

> And sport, Sweet Maid, in season of these years,
> And learn to gather flowers before they wither—

But indeed if Shakespeare's sonnets are excepted and a very few other poems, all sixteenth century love poetry is made after Horace's receipt:

> Let now the chimneys blaze
> And cups o'erflow with wine;
> Let well-tuned words amaze
> With harmony divine.
> Now yellow waxen lights
> Shall wait on honey love—

That is Horace's lover's paradise and he himself could have described it no more exactly.

Common sense is perhaps not necessarily destructive to the imagination, but on most of the soaring flights your truly inspired poet essays it would prove a dragging weight. Horace never soared at all. He was the least inspired of poets and he was contentedly aware that he was. He admired Virgil exceedingly and other lofty epic and tragic poets of the day whose names alone have come down to us, but for himself he wanted only the pleasant ways of earth. He esteemed—more, one feels sure, than he loved—the mighty Greek masters, and he bade young writers turn their pages all the day long and the night, but he never swerved from what his cool head showed him was his own little path, serenely sure those heights were not for him: "Like a river rushing from the mountain, on sweeps Pindar, deep-mouthed, tremendous . . . [or] a mighty wind lifts him aloft into the region of the clouds. I am like the bee that busy works in the sweet wild thyme around the groves and banks of wide-watered Tibur. Even so small and toiling hard like her I build my songs."

This attitude toward his work is typical of him. Never was

there a poet of fewer pretensions, and yet with all his gay self-depreciation he knew his powers and that he had "raised a monument more lasting than brass and higher than the crumbling magnificence of pyramids," and that he would be read—the words in their unintentional understatement are almost ironical—"as long as pontifex and vestal virgin climbed to the Capitol."

A few times this consciousness of his genius overcomes the habit of his genuine modesty, but only once or twice. With more pretentiousness and greater self-assurance he would not have been the completely delightful person he was. His genius must be taken on faith by all who cannot read him in the original, but anyone who cares to run through the poorest translation will perceive something of his delightfulness. No misdirected efforts on the part of a translator can quite prevent that from coming through.

To begin with, he was that charming contradiction, a man who enjoyed luxury and yet was completely independent of it. The choice bouquet of an old wine was never wasted upon his palate nor the extraordinary recherché dishes of the day which would seem to have been an epicure's paradise. Horace knew all about the superiority of a chicken drowned in wine to one killed in the usual way, of game caught in mild weather rather than cold, of fruit plucked while the moon was on the wane, and precisely when in the composition of a fish sauce Greek wine should be used. But this exquisiteness amused him far more than it pleased him and he liked best "My own pot of leeks and pease with a thin bit of bread and only three slaves [!] to serve me. A white stone table where two bowls stand with the mixing vessel [the wine was mixed with water, often sea water, to give a tang like Apollinaris], a pitcher and a platter of common earthenware. Thence care-free to sleep and lie abed till ten, with no business to send me early abroad. . . . So I live more sweetly than the greatest of the earth."

This sort of thing, repeated again and again, has not a touch of affectation. It is not the luxury-sated, blasé man about town, sentimentalizing over what nothing would induce him to try. It is the very reverse of this, the freedom given by a mind which can find securely the source of pleasure within and needs no outside stimulus—except, to be sure, a cup of wine or, rather, many cups. On this point Horace would have admitted no opposition. He had the most positive convictions on wine's virtue as well as its delights. "No songs can please nor yet live long which are written by those who drink water"; "Plant no tree before the sacred vine, O Varus. To the dry all things are hard by God's ordainment"; "O jar of wine born when I was born, worthy to be brought forth on a glad day, come out now to us, O gentle spur of the spirit, without you harsh and hard to move." It is the subject of his most impassioned verse.

Still, any *vino del paese* was good enough for him, so he always protested, and when Maecenas gave him a country place—Horace's Sabine Farm, the most famous farm in literature, his more than pleasure, his unalloyed delight, in plainest country living overflows in poem after poem: "This was among my prayers: a portion of land, not so big, a garden and near the house a spring of never-failing water, and a little wood beyond. The gods have done more and better. It is well. I ask no more." But he can never have done writing about it: "Not ivory nor gold in fretted ceilings shine in my house, not marble from Hymettus. . . . Nothing beyond what I have do I ask, blessed in my one, my only Sabine farm." It was his "corner of earth that smiled at him before all others." He prays to "the lord of the curved lyre": "What does his poet ask of Apollo enshrined? Not rich grain lands in fertile Sardinia, not gold nor ivory of India. Olives are my fare and tender herbs from field and garden. O Son of Latona, give me to enjoy what is mine—and with unweakened mind an old age not uncomely or deprived of poetry." "There are those who have not," he wrote. "There is one who does not care to have."

This attitude of moderation was his by nature; it was also in accordance with his reasoned convictions. He was not a man who lived carelessly on the surface. That was his way only in his love affairs. He was a serious observer of life. Temperamentally he was

inclined to be happy and he wanted happiness intensely, but by a
necessity of his nature he could find it only if he thought things
through. He had to have some secure basis to build upon; he
could not and would not feel himself the sport of a blind chance
he had no defense against. That way lay unreasoning misery for
him and he refused to acquiesce miserably in an existence that was
not reasonable. He insisted upon finding sense in the way things
are, and so a possibility of living serenely through life's cares and
troubles, difficulties and dangers. It was the impulse which plays
a great part in religion. It is true that Horace was far from what
we think of as a religious nature. Strange thoughts that transcend
our wonted themes and into glory peep were never for a moment
his. He knew nothing about mystic heights as a man any more
than he did as a poet, but he had a religion, although it was constructed by common sense alone and adapted to satisfy only its
sober demands.

Of formal religion in Rome at that time there was little left,
and nothing at all that could make a rational appeal. The
emperor was almost at the point of being the one true effective
god. But Greek thought had found its way to Rome. There had
come seekers for truth in the Platonic fashion, not from lovely
visions of deities incarnate in woodland, river and sea, but from
what men found within themselves. Out of these philosophies
Horace took what suited him and he laid a foundation he could
build his life upon.

Happiness and misery, he said to himself, are inside emotions,
not outside facts; essentially, then, they are under my control. I
can do nothing about what fate sends me, but I can do everything
about the way I take what is sent. I can so order my own spirit
that no matter how outrageous fortune is I can keep my balance
within unmoved. "Do you know, friend, what I feel, for what I
pray? Not to waver to and fro, hanging upon the hope of the
dubious hour. God may give this or that—life—wealth. I will my
own self make my spirit undisturbed."

There lies the whole secret of life. The only important matter is what we are. "The fool," he writes, "finds fault with a place. The fault is not there but in the mind, and that can never escape from itself." It is his underlying thought, expressed in countless ways; "They change their sky, but not their mind, who run across the sea. The thing you seek is here, in every meanest village, if a balanced and serene temper does not fail you." Always he urges, "Prepare what will make you a friend to your own self."

And the receipt to secure this even balance, this equanimity— a word made up from the two Latin words Horace uses to express the idea—is to live within careful limits, to contract one's desires, to forgo mountain tops and perilous ecstasies, and choose forever and always safety first. This is Horace's creed of "golden mediocrity," which he who practices will be secure alike from the envy threatening great palaces and—since he will never take a risk— from the danger of helpless, sordid poverty. For life's voyage shorten sail, no matter what the wind. "Even," he writes, "the wise man is a fool if he seeks virtue itself beyond what is enough."

So, in perfect poise, undistracted by hope or fear, a man can fully live where every one of us must, whether we will or not and no matter how hard we let the future press upon us, in this very present, passing moment. "He is master of himself and happy who as the day ends can say, I have lived—tomorrow come cloud, come sunshine. Not Jove himself can blot out one single deed that lies behind, nor can he ever bring to naught or make undone what once the flying hour has borne away." The only sure thing in life is death, "pale death, which knocks with equal hand at poor men's hovels and the towers of kings," and "life's brief space forbids long hope." Then "Believe that each dawn brings your last day to you," and "Why not beneath a tall plane tree or this pine here recline at ease, roses to wreathe the hair and perfumes of Araby to give sweet scents. Boy, be swift to quench the fire of the wine-cup with water from the stream gliding by, and fetch us Lyde. Bid her make haste with her ivory lyre." Horace had noted well Catullus' words to Lesbia and he could echo them from his heart: "The swift moons can repair their losses in the sky. We, when we are gone where the great dead have passed, are dust and shadow. Who knows if the gods will add tomorrow to today."

That is Horace's philosophy and, in general, the religion of the man of the world. It is a sad religion, for all its emphasis upon Lyde and her lyre and the pleasant river bank. He who embraces it sincerely will always be able to command a merry spirit for others, but his own self melancholy will claim. There is no combination more attractive. The underlying sadness tempers the gaiety to something gentle and infinitely endearing. It is genuinely gay; any appeal for pity, however subtle, would be ruinous, but always it suggests a spirit that is gallant to look at darkness undismayed, but deeply, sorrowfully regretful that fate has so ordained. This is the innermost secret of Horace's never-failing charm, the reason, more than all his felicities of words and measures, why the generations since have loved him as his own did. One of his devoted admirers wrote soon after his death: "Admit him and he plays around your heart"—plays always, but always close to the heart.

And yet, deplorable contradiction, never was poet such an inveterate preacher. Poetry and preaching do not go well together; when the preacher mounts the pulpit the poet usually goes away. Horace was not aware of this fact; no Roman was. The Roman idea was that the more a man preached, provided he did it with due regard to metrical considerations, the greater poet he was. Morality in rolling hexameters was poetry's highest achievement, along with patriotism, of course. How far preaching came natural to Horace, how far Rome thrust it upon him, no one now can know. As a Roman who was a poet he must press his poetry into the service of the state and urge citizens on to their duty. One does not really resent his doing so in the *Satires* and *Epistles*. He writes them avowedly as a teacher and often he teaches very pleasantly and wisely. But in his odes it is enraging in the midst of lovely poetry to come upon this sort of thing: "The centuries, fertile in vice, have debased marriage and the race and the home. Derived from this source ruin has overflowed country and people. The grown girl delights to be taught the movements of the voluptuous dance." Or, "Now few acres are left for the plough by the great mass of regal buildings. . . . Not thus was it ordered when Romulus ruled or unshaven Cato or by the maxims of the ancients. Their private list of possessions was short, the common wealth was great." Or, "Force devoid of intelligence falls by its own weight," and so on, with all the excellent results force under wise control can produce. A great deal about how the world is running down until by now there is little hope left for it: "Our parents, worse than our grandparents, gave birth to us who are worse than they, and we shall in our turn bear offspring still more evil."

It would be hard to find in the whole of Greek literature as much preaching as Horace does all by himself. Euripides saw war as completely evil and he wrote the greatest anti-war piece of literature there is, the *Trojan Women*, but from first to last he never mounts the pulpit. He never denounces war at all; he only shows what it is. The preacher, full-fledged, arrived in literature with the Romans. Even Plautus, so averse to it by nature, had now and then to assume the office. Terence took eagerly to it and so did Cicero. But Horace, in proportion to the rest of his writing, more than they all. There was a mighty moulding force at work to make this singer of lovely songs, this gay and humorous spirit, this mind of serene detachment, into the earnest denouncer of vice and exhorter to virtue. Rome was back of Horace. And yet, though one may wish a kinder fate had placed him in Athens in her prime, there is a warm and winning quality in his eagerness to do his bit in helping Augustus turn the empire back to the good old ways and create again a plain-living, high-acting Rome. We look with awe upon the great Greek tragedians who seem hardly aware of mere mortality. Horace plays around our heart. The Greek poets are our masters; the Latin poets are our own familiar friends.

IX

The Rome of Augustus as Horace Saw It

Through the streets of the great city Horace strolled, cocking an amused eye at a fashionable lady's short dress, at a perfumed young elegant's latest thing in the way of togas, at the bearers of a great personage's litter—no carriages were allowed in the streets during the day—at his own slave on tip-toe to scan eagerly a poster of a gladiatorial show, at a grand funeral procession preceded by blaring brass horns and trumpets, and with especial delight at a fastidious poet's latest effusion hung outside the book shop where it was being pawed over by the sweaty hands of the vulgar. He stopped before a famous painter's work in a portico—there were miles of these roofed colonnades—had a look at a merchant's stock of "pearls from farthest Arabia and India, giver of wealth"; at other shops where could be bought "silver and antique marble and bronze and works of art, jewels and Tyrian purple," rare and beautiful things from everywhere in the world. "The Tiber," a writer in the next generation wrote, "is the most placid merchant of all that is produced over the whole earth."

But the splendor was only part of the spectacle. The crowd—Horace's abhorrence, "I hate the common herd and keep them off"—is so dense, he must "push and struggle and knock aside the slow," while they shout after him with jeering impudence, "what are you after, you crazy fellow, thinking you must knock down whatever stands in your way if you're hurrying to Maecenas." The description, brief as it is, is full of significance. Rome was a very big city by then, but the words leave no doubt that poets were

highly interesting objects there. Even the vulgar recognized
Horace as he passed on his way and knew perfectly where he was
probably going. It is clear, too, that if the crowd was not man-
nerly and good tempered, it was not submissive and servile either.
Never in Rome did the rank and file—those above the slave-class,
of course—reach the condition of helpless insignificance to which
Europe again and again saw the common people reduced. The city
crowd was something the most magnificent emperor must bear in
mind. Romans, penniless, in rags, however reduced, were a force
to be reckoned with. No other proletariat in all history ever got
free food for themselves and free shows too.

In the satire quoted, Horace has been to call on a man who
lives on the Aventine and now must make his way to the Quirinal:
"You see how convenient the distance is for a mere mortal." (It
meant a four-mile walk up and down hill.) "Every one is abroad.
A canny contractor hurries by with his mules and porters; here a
derrick is hoisting now a rock, now a huge beam; sad funerals
struggle to pass on; there a mad dog is running away; next comes
a muddy pig." The words are a clear little vignette of a street-
scene in that city which is so familiar to us and yet really so little
known. They put Rome before us, her very self, as she would look
if a view of her could be flashed for a moment upon the silver
screen.

All over the world and in every age a great city is a place of
contrasts, but Rome was so, as even an Oriental city could hardly
be today. The inner balance of the spirit was precious to Horace
because all outside was unbalanced. During the empire the pen-
dulum swung in ever wider and wider sweeps, but even in his day
extremes had become the rule of life. On top absolute despotism,
at bottom well-nigh hopeless slavery; splendid luxury and
unspeakable squalor; monstrous forms of irresponsible pleasure
and fearful misery—everywhere violent oppositions. Harmony
had been the Greek ideal, life within and without in equilibrium;
the world seen as beautiful and the spirit at home in it. To the

Roman this idea was forever incomprehensible. Horace, akin in many ways to the Greek, never imagined such a condition even to the degree of longing for it. His search was not to adjust himself to life—nor life to himself, but to find within himself the good, which was in direct contradiction to life. The sharp division between facts, things, all that the Roman called reality exactly as we do today, and the ideas and ideals within a man was never sharper than during the Roman Empire. To Horace and his kind there were two distinct worlds, one without and one within; they were not seen as related.

Horace's Rome is first of all a place where money rules— "Queen Money" is his phrase. He who cared little for it by nature, lived in an atmosphere so permeated by it, that it is perpetually on his lips; the age, as it were, superinduced an attitude alien to Horace himself. Here is a notable change from the age of Cicero, distant by so short a space of actual time. Horace as a boy must often have had the great orator pointed out to him. But in Cicero money is completely in the background; it is almost never mentioned. Cicero was a lover of the good things of life it can buy as Horace was not; money was actually far more important to him. The different part it plays in the writings of each is due only to the difference between the aristocrat and the self-made man. Cicero, not by birth, nor indeed by nature, but perfectly by acquisition, had the tone of the old republican aristocracy where money was taken for granted and never talked about. Why should it be? It was always there and no more interesting as a subject of conversation than the tides of the sea or any other fixed phenomenon of nature. But all that was changed with the coming of Augustus. No intelligent despot allows an old aristocracy to continue. Very skillfully, very swiftly and with complete finality the great families of Rome were removed to the far background. In the society Horace was familiar with there was no settled class of any sort. The man who got rich got all the other prizes, too; he was the one to be admired and emulated and chosen for office. His birth mattered not at all. He might be a freedman, born a slave, with no tradition behind him and no education to fit him for high responsibilities. Horace delights in holding up to scorn the vulgar new-made millionaire to whose exquisite dinners men of fashion and men of letters will flock and as they enjoy his chef's triumphs, make use of their napkins to conceal irrepressible amusement at their host's ostentatious display.

There are two curious little letters among his *Epistles* which illustrate better than anything else he wrote how all-important money had become. In each of them he tells a young man how to better his fortunes, and the advice he gives is to make friends with the rich. A morose Greek philosopher, Horace observes, may say, "If I can live contentedly on poor fare, I can dispense with people who have money," but a wiser view of life is that of the man who says, "If I can make use of people who have money, I can dispense with poor fare." In point of fact, he declares, the latter is really the one to be respected, the man of energy and enterprise, who is determined to get on and will not sit down lazily, contented with a little. He ends his letter with a warning to be tactful: Those who are silent about their poverty in the presence of the rich get more than he who keeps asking. Remember to take modestly and not be greedy, even though the end and aim of your friendship is to be enriched. In the second letter which is addressed, seriously, without a touch of irony, to "Lollius, most independent of men," he writes that the inexperienced are apt to think it will be a simple matter to cultivate a powerful friend, but the man who has tried it knows there are many hazards. Lollius must above all guard against that independence of his. If the great man wants to go a-hunting, up with you; leave your bed; put by your books; yield always to his wishes. As he is grave or gay so do you be, nor for heaven's sake when he feels like doing something else, try to read him poetry. The concluding exhortation, that while the young man is making himself agreeable, he must not forget to cultivate his higher powers by the study of philosophy, is also spoken in all seriousness and with no idea of irony.

They are illuminating letters. One can see the young men, faced with the problem of what they are to do, asking advice from a conspicuously successful older friend to whose career they are inclining. Horace's father had been born a slave; he himself was ranked with the great, and the reason was that he had made himself acceptable to a rich and powerful man. No one who reads him can doubt that he had a deep affection for Maecenas. It appears, indeed, to have been the great affection of his life, but to his worldly common sense friendship with the rich as a career had nothing to do with the emotions. He would never have been guilty of the sentimentality of urging the young men to love those whose dependents they became. There was no hypocrisy in him ever. The methods he recommended to them were undoubtedly those he had himself practiced toward Maecenas; what he had felt while doing so, his genuine devotion, seemed to him quite beside the point. It was all a clear matter of business. It never entered his mind that there was anything objectionable in a show of devotion for the purpose of getting money from a man. Nature did not originally incline the Roman character to servility. Horace and his young friends were the product of an age where it was important so far beyond everything else to have a good deal of money, and where it had become so difficult to get it, that the sense of honor in its pursuit had been lost even to a man like Horace, in other ways highly honorable.

Money under one guise or another appears perpetually in his writing. The miser, now almost dropped from literature, plays a large part. He was evidently a most familiar figure in Augustan days and Horace knows his readers will not blame him for exaggeration when he shows him hardly willing to spend a few pennies from his great hoard on medicine necessary to save his life. And, of course, side by side with him is his invariable foil, the spendthrift and the gambler. Money always, well to the fore.

"Everything," is Horace's ironical summary, "virtue, honor, fame, everything human and divine, obey beautiful riches. He who has heaped them up is renowned, brave, just. A wise man, too? Yes, and a king."

Throughout the poems, too, keep recurring the things money can buy, all manner of expensiveness, ivory couches, mosaic floors, hangings of Tyrian purple, embroideries, inlay, rare antiques, jewels, silver dishes, golden vases, in complete contrast to Greek literature where furniture and furnishings play no part at all. It is as impossible to conceive of Pindar's describing the menu and the dining table of Hieron of Sicily, his familiar host and, no doubt, a sovereign surrounded by magnificence, or of Plato in the *Symposium* moved either to admiration or disapproval by Agathon's tablecloth, as it is to think of Horace apart from his keen interest in the way people did their houses and served their dinner parties. It is true that he never praised luxury or enjoyed it much, but he was always keenly aware of it. Agathon and his guests no doubt ate carelessly what was set before them and took all the details incidental to the meal with complete indifference as a matter of course. But who could take it as a matter of course if he saw as Horace did, a slave enter the dining room bearing a peacock roasted in its feathers, the gorgeous tail outspread, so that the glowing creature looked as if it had but alighted for a moment on the silver dish? Or when a whole boar, bending the great platter with its weight, was presented to the company? In the eyes of Plato's Athenian gentlemen a dinner party was chiefly an occasion for conversation; to Horace's friends it was a matter of spectacular display and extraordinarily elaborate and overwhelmingly abundant food.

Cooking and serving and bills of fare occupy a great deal of Horace's attention. No less than the whole of two poems, and long ones at that, and the half of another are about nothing else: *Horace:* "How did you fare at the grand dinner party?" *Friend:* "Never better in my life." *Horace:* "Do tell me if it won't bore you, what were the hors d'oeuvres?" And a hundred lines follow which make fun of the menu, indeed, but give it nevertheless in greatest detail, together with a number of receipts for cooking the especially delicious dishes. On that occasion those Roman gentlemen ate: cold wild boar with all sorts of pickled vegetables; oysters and shell fish with a marvellous sauce; two varieties of turbot; a wonderful dish where a great fish seemed to be swimming among shrimp, with a relish made of fish from Spain, wine from Greece, vinegar from Lesbos and white pepper; then wild fowl served with corn; the liver of a white goose fattened on ripe figs; shoulder of hare ("so much more succulent than the lower part"); broiled black birds and wood pigeons. Sweets are not mentioned and of fruit only bright red apples, but elsewhere Horace speaks of dainties for dessert as beneath the attention of a true epicure and advises a final course of black mulberries—but they must be gathered before the sun is high.

"We rise from table," he remarks, "pale from over-eating," and the modern reader understands why the early Christians put gluttony among the seven deadly sins. The practice of using emetics to make more and more eating possible seems to have become the fashion only at a later date. Horace does not mention it and it is so exactly the sort of thing he most enjoyed holding up to scorn, he would never have passed it over. But to those who desire to understand the quality of Rome it offers a profitable subject for meditation.

Indeed, along with the elegance and even magnificence of Horace's dinner parties there might be on occasion a lack of the most ordinary decency. Horace was so aware of tablecloths because they were so often dirty, exceedingly dirty. He sends an invitation to a friend with the promise that if he will come and dine with him neither cloth nor napkins will be in such a condition as to make him wrinkle his nose in disgust. Why should such things be, he laments, when cleanliness is so easy and so cheap. All the same, he ends the letter with the simple statement that his guest may count on plenty of room at table and not fear objectionable odors, as happens when people are seated too close to one another. And this is Rome of the stupendous Roman baths.

With those urbane gentlemen of the great Augustan age coarseness lay just beneath the polished surface and often it came out on top. If a friend reclining next him at table, Horace writes, drinks rather too much, lets fall the precious old china, then does unprintable—in English—things, and lastly leans across him and snatches away his piece of chicken, will he hold him less dear or less agreeable on that account? No, indeed, the reader is swift to conclude. Horace and the people he was writing for were perfectly accustomed to these little *faux pas* and had only a tolerant smile for them.

Horace went a journey once with some very great personages. Maecenas was one of them and "the most learned of Greeks" another, two prominent diplomats also, of whom Horace describes one as "an exquisite finished to a hair," and three well-known men of letters, Virgil among them. It was a distinguished company such as the world has not often seen. Three of them after nineteen hundred years are still familiar household names. On their way a night is spent at a friend's villa where they are entertained while at dinner by a little play, a dialogue between "Sarmentus, a buffoon, and Messius, nicknamed the Cock," the former, as appears, a thin little man and the latter a huge, phenomenally ugly peasant. This was the diversion they offered that gathering: *Sarmentus:* "I say, you're like a wild horse" (laughter from the audience). *Messius* (shaking his head ferociously): "So I am— Look out." *Sarmentus* (eyes fixed on a hideous great hairy scar that marks Messius' forehead): "Aha, if your horn hadn't been cut out from your head, what wouldn't you do, if you threaten like that, all mutilated." He goes on to press the point still nearer home by jokes on the kind of diseases that leave such disfigurements and on Messius' pleasant vices, and the big man is urged to "dance the Cyclops" for the company, as he looks just like one.

But he on his side scores as well: "Oh, you—you're just a slave. Whatever made you run away from your mistress? It couldn't be because she starved you—why, you're tiny enough to grow fat on next to nothing." It *was* a delightful entertainment, Horace concludes. And the grave and witty gentlemen of the *Symposium* come to mind, who dismiss the flute girl and her "noise" so that they may have no disturbance in the entertainment they want for their dinner of high discourse.

Of course the comparison is not quite fair: Horace is apparently recounting what really did happen, Plato probably only imagining what might have; all the same, it holds good fundamentally as regards the quality of the Greek and the Roman. "Tell me how you amuse yourself and I will tell you what you are." The very élite of Rome made up that little gathering who were so diverted by the clowning and the diseases and the big hairy scar. They were for the Augustan age what Socrates and Aristophanes and the others in the *Symposium* were for the age of Pericles, and it is difficult to think of any of the Athenians transferred to the Roman table finding much amusement there. Ugliness and deformity and disease were not the subjects Aristophanes chose for his jokes, nor was he given to dialogue of the "you're another and worse too" variety. And Horace and Virgil at the Greek supper would very soon have been bored by the long speeches about nothing real in all the world. That kind of fine-spun theorizing would have seemed to them a pure waste of time, neither pleasurable nor profitable. Horace has given us his ideal of first-rate talk: "Let us discuss what is important to us, not other people's houses or villas or whether Lepos dances badly or not, but whether riches or virtue make men happy, and whether motives of right or utility should influence us in seeking friends." Conversation of that kind, a Roman thought, got people somewhere. It helped them to be good citizens. If they wanted to be amused, there were the fools and the clowns and the gladiators too.

None of the dinners Horace describes were enlivened by the

spectacle of a pair of men or several pairs, fighting to kill each other, with the divertissement a failure if neither of them did. These were the invention of a later day, but to public gladiatorial contests Rome had been accustomed for two hundred years and more before Horace's time, and it is hardly surprising that he found nothing to object to in them. He was in good company: Cicero took them as complacently. Horace never indeed describes a fight or speaks of having been present at one, but gladiators he mentions more than once and always in as matter-of-fact a way as he would an actor or a singer. In one of his Satires he reports a little talk with Maecenas, where in between a question as to what o'clock it is and a remark about the weather, they discuss the chances of two favorites billed to fight each other: "Is the Chicken with Thracian armour (a very small shield) a match for Syrus?"

It goes without saying that he never took note of slaves, but it is worthy of remark that a man sensitive and quick of feeling as he was should write of their terrible punishments with complete unconcern. He does say mildly that a man who has a slave crucified because he stole a bit of food must be out of his mind, but he speaks of slaves being beaten as a matter of course, of "the horrible scourge," with pieces of metal attached to the lashes, and of others of the methods of torture devised to keep in order a class grown dangerous because of its enormous size. A man of position, says Horace, is mean if he walks out with only five slaves attending him; on the other hand, one who can be seen with two hundred has passed the limit of good sense. And yet in spite of their great numbers they were so completely without any human significance, so casually mistreated and murdered in that city accustomed by all the favorite forms of amusement to mortal agony and violent death, that their condition never drew a passing thought from even the very best, a man like Horace, a thinker, gentle, kindly, dutiful. His bewilderment, if he could be recalled to life and confronted with our point of view, would be pitiful. He was wise and good, yet he lived with a monstrous evil and never caught a glimpse of it. So does custom keep men blinded.

In certain other respects, however, important too, our way would seem quite familiar to the Romans, more by far than the Greek way. Socrates in the *Symposium*, when Alcibiades challenged him to drink two quarts of wine, could have done so or not as he chose, but the diners-out of Horace's day had no such freedom. He speaks often of the master of the drinking, who was always appointed to dictate how much each man was to drink. Very many unseemly dinner parties must have paved the way for that regulation. A Roman in his cups would have been hard to handle, surly, quarrelsome, dangerous. No doubt there had been banquets without number which had ended in fights, broken furniture, injuries, deaths. Pass a law then, the invariable Roman remedy, to keep drunkenness within bounds. Of course it worked both ways: everybody was obliged to empty the same number of glasses and the temperate man had to drink a great deal more than he wanted, but whenever laws are brought in to regulate the majority who have not abused their liberty for the sake of the minority who have, just such unexpected results come to pass. Indeed, any attempt to establish a uniform average in that stubbornly individual phenomenon, human nature, will have only one result that can be foretold with certainty: it will press hardest upon the best, as everyone knows who is driven by large numbers to use mass methods.

The Athenian idea was that a gentleman could be left free and trusted not to get obnoxious to others over his wine. The Roman idea was that he assuredly could not be, but that he could and should be kept in order. Harmony, said the Athenian. Freedom, because the good life was in conformity with a man's innermost desires. Discipline, said the Roman. Careful regulation, because the good life must be imposed upon human nature that desired evil.

Horace deplored the drinking laws: "O country, when shall I

see you. O nights and feasts of the gods where each, free from absurd rules, may drink as he pleases." And it did not escape his keen vision that all law was an empty form unless the moral feeling of the people was back of it. Nevertheless through his poems as through Roman literature there is discernible always, expressed or implicit, the sense of life controlled and ordered by stern outside forces, along with the law "the adamantine nails of dire Necessity," the inexorable decrees of Jove, Fate that spins and cuts the thread at will. "Must" is constantly on Horace's lips. "This you must do—must submit to—must face—must endure." So Romans saw life, and with all Horace's search for freedom within, he was not able ever to feel that he was free.

Catullus is the notable exception. "The dread goddess, Necessity" had no place among his deities. He saw his life in his own hands—and Lesbia's, but then high passion is never aware of any necessity other than its own, and except for Catullus, high passion is the rarest of visitants in Roman literature.

Such are the outstanding features in Horace's miniature of Rome, but what he leaves out of it has significance too. The political game which took up all the foreground for Cicero is not there at all. The result foreshadowed by the condition in Cicero's day came to pass: the citizen body could not cope with its own corruption; the frightful evils that followed had to be terminated; hence a dictator, with all the responsibility and all power to regulate everything in the state. And the many brilliant and able men of the great Augustan age drew deep breaths of relief at seeing themselves freed from trouble and concern about public matters to devote themselves to their own business. They had been angrily impatient of the dishonesty and stupidity and inefficiency of the Republic's officials. They were sick to death of the wars and the mismanagement of home affairs, foreign affairs, and miscarriages of justice. That was ended now. A strong and sagacious man was emperor, whose will was the only law that counted, and Romans rejoiced. What lay before their country in the future, the most irresponsible despotism the western world has ever seen, they could not know; nor were they interested to build for the future. That kind of disinterested patriotism was dead in Rome and would not rise again except here and there in a few men, so few they never mattered at all.

In one of Horace's *Epistles* there is a little description of the theatre as he knew it, which seems to stand in brief, not indeed for him or his group, but for the general spirit of the day, as the popular theatre does stand always and everywhere: "The people, even while the actors are speaking the verses, call for a bear show or a wrestling match. Pleasure has moved away from the ear to the restless eye and entertainment with no meaning. For four hours or more the curtain is up, while troops of horsemen fly past and hordes of footmen. Kings of fallen fortune are dragged in with hands bound behind the back. War chariots hasten by, carts, carriages, ships, ivory is borne along and all the spoils of Corinth. That hybrid creature, the giraffe, then catches the crowd's attention or, it may be, a white elephant. And what actors' voices are strong enough to rise above the din? The spectators ask each other, 'Has the actor said anything yet?' 'I don't think so.' 'What are you so pleased with then?' 'Oh, that beautiful purple dress of his.'"

The spectacle, ever growing more and more varied and more and more gorgeous, was what Rome by now wanted. Not what satisfied the mind nor yet the spirit, but what satisfied the restless eye. Rome's importance was her size and her wealth and her power. Roman citizens' lives consisted in the abundance of the things that they possessed. To Pericles, Athens' glory was not the Parthenon, not the Acropolis, but that Athens had become the school of Greece in all ways of wisdom. Augustus' title to glory, repeated over and over again, was that he had found Rome a city of brick and left her a city of marble.

X

The Roman Way

"To the people of Romulus I set no fixed goal to achievement," Virgil makes Jupiter in the *Æneid* say of Rome's future glory, "no end to empire. I have given them authority without limit." Unlimited is what the Romans were, in desires, in ambitions, in appetites, as well as in power and extent of empire. There is a note of exaggeration in Rome, contradicting on first sight the outstanding national quality of practical sagacity which made them great empire builders. But upon closer view it ceases to be a contradiction. The Romans were pre-eminently men of war. The only choice they had for centuries was to conquer or be conquered. Possibly war was their most natural expression; certainly it was the price they must pay for being a nation. Under the spur of its desperate necessities in eight hundred years of fighting, as Livy reckons them, from the founding of the city to his own day, they developed extraordinarily one side of their genius, a sure, keen-sighted, steady common sense, but war, with its alternations of stern repression and orgies of rapine and plunder, was not a training to modify violent desires. Always rude, primitive, physical appetites were well to the fore.

What constitutes Rome's greatness, in the last analysis, is that powerful as these were in her people there was something still more powerful; ingrained in them was the idea of discipline, the soldier's fundamental idea. However fierce the urge of their nature was, the feeling for law and order was deeper, the deepest thing in them. Their outbreaks were terrible; civil wars such as our world has not seen again; dealings with conquered enemies which are a fearful page in history. Nevertheless, the outstanding fact about Rome is her unwavering adherence to the idea of a controlled life, subject not to this or that individual, but to a system embodying the principles of justice and fair dealing.

How savage the Roman nature was which the Roman law controlled is seen written large in Rome's favorite amusements, too familiar to need more than a cursory mention: wild beast hunts— so-called, the hunting place was the arena; naval battles for which the circus was flooded by means of hidden canals; and, most usual and best loved by the people, the gladiators, when the great amphitheatre was packed close tier upon tier, all Rome there to see human beings by the tens and hundreds killing each other, to give the victor in a contest the signal for death and eagerly watch the upraised dagger plunge into the helpless body and the blood spurt forth.

That was Rome's dearest delight and her unique contribution to the sport of the world. None of these spectacles were Greek. They entered Greece only under Roman leadership and Athens, it is claimed, never allowed gladiators. Twice, we are told, the citizens stopped a fight as it was about to begin, both times aroused by the protest of a great man. "Athenians," cried one of them, "before you admit the gladiators, come with me and destroy the altar to Pity," and the people with one voice declared that their theatre should never be so defiled. The second time, a revered and beloved philosopher denounced the brutality they were about to witness, and the result was the same. But everywhere else Rome went the bloody games followed, and all the time they grew more bloody and more extravagant. On one occasion we read of a hundred lions perishing and as many lionesses. On another, five thousand animals were killed, bulls, tigers, panthers, elephants. The poet Martial, who wrote endless epigrams to flatter the great Vespasian's son, the Emperor Domitian, some seventy-five years after Augustus, says: "The hunter by the Ganges has not to fear in the countries of the Orient as many tigers as Rome has seen. This city can no longer count her joys.

Caesar, your arena surpasses the triumph and splendor of Bacchus whose car only two tigers draw."

Of how many human beings met their death in these ways no estimate at all can be made. The supply of prisoners of war could not begin to meet the demand and men condemned to die were sent to help fill the gladiatorial schools, as they were called; masters, too, often sold their slaves to them; there were even volunteers. Cicero speaks of these more than once. As the games went on, the exaggeration in every direction resulted in what seems to the modern reader incredible, the creations of a monstrous fantasy. We hear of the arena being sprinkled with gold dust; of dwarfs matched against each other and against wild beasts; women, too. Martial tells of having seen a woman kill a lion. Emperors fought, in carefully arranged contests, of course. The son of Rome's best ruler, Marcus Aurelius, boasted that he had killed or conquered two thousand gladiators, using his left hand only. The account ends by growing monotonous. Human ingenuity in devising new and more diverting ways of slaughter was finally exhausted and all that could be done to satisfy the impatient spectators was to increase the number engaged. In one naval battle when the arena was flooded, it is recorded that twenty-four ships took part, large enough to hold in all nineteen thousand men.

It is impossible to escape the suspicion, as one reads description after description, that journalese was not unknown in Rome. Surely, the reader is driven to reason, a people with a tendency to exaggeration would not always successfully repress it on a subject that almost irresistibly invited it, even though they claimed to be writing accurate historical records. When finally one is told of an emperor in the later days of the empire who "would never dine without human blood," without, that is, watching men kill each other, suspicion becomes a certainty. It is too perfectly the tabloid newspaper headline. How could such a fact be known? The gossip of palace slaves? Or even the assertion of the imperial brute himself, wanting, as a Roman would, to appear to out-Nero Nero?

Especially monstrous events in the games and especially enormous numbers of those killed in them are hardly to be accepted
as plain history, but they do show what Aristotle called the truth
which is truer than history. Romans wrote them for Romans, and
Romans enjoyed reading and believing them.

To pass from this contemplation, from the way Rome was
pleased to amuse herself, to the consideration of what she really
did in the world, is to make a startling transition. The Romans
did not trample all nations down before them in ruthless brutality
and kill and kill in a savage lust for blood. They created a great
civilization. Rome's monumental achievement, never effaced from
the world, was law. A people violent by nature, of enormous
appetites and brutal force, produced the great Law of Nations
which sustained with equal justice the rights of free-born men
everywhere. The fact with all its familiarity has the power to
astonish whenever it comes to mind, but the reasons are easily to
be seen. The little town on the seven hills conquered the other little towns around her, because her citizens could obey orders. No
one who knows Rome at all will feel this a mere conjecture. The
father who condemned his son to death for winning a victory
against orders is a legendary figure of deep significance. The orgy
of the arena was a relaxation, in the same way as destroying a captured city was or a murderous civil outbreak. They were incidental merely. The conception of a power outside themselves to
which they must and would submit was enduring. Over the law-
less earth where petty tribes were forever fighting other petty
tribes for the right to live, where there was nothing more enlight-
ened than tribal customs untold ages old, marched the Roman,
bringing with him as certainly as his sword and his lance his idea
of an ordered life in which no man and no tribe was free, but all
bound to obey an impersonal, absolute authority which imposed
the necessity of self-controlled action. Along with the tremendous
Roman roads and aqueducts went the ideal of which they were the
symbol, civilization, founded and upheld by law.

The conception was magnificent, grandiose. It was Rome who spread wherever she went the great idea that a man must be assumed to be innocent until he was proved to be guilty; who pronounced it the height of injustice to carry any law out logically without regard to the practical good or ill which resulted; who never in her law-making quite lost sight of the conception that all, men or women, free or slaves, were "by nature" equal.

The civilization that resulted showed again and again the strength which no mere external force, however powerful, ever possesses. The Gauls were fierce fighters, people of high spirit, undisciplined too, but when once they had experienced what Roman civilization meant, its superiority was so evident, they never after Caesar's conquest had any general uprising against the Roman rule. The Acts of the Apostles gives a wonderful picture of what it meant to belong to Rome. St. Paul, though a Jew of Tarsus, was yet a Roman, so the record states, the little Asia Minor city having been admitted to the Roman federation. In a town where he was preaching, the magistrates, induced by the Jews, seized him and ordered him to be scourged, but just before they did so Paul cried out that he was a Roman citizen, and they sent word to their officer, "Take heed what thou doest, for he is a Roman." Then "the chief captain came and asked him, Art thou a Roman? He said, Yea. And the chief captain answered, With a great sum obtained I this freedom. And Paul said, But I was born free." The proud words received their due: St. Paul under strong escort was sent away from the town where his enemies were determined to kill him, to the Roman governor of the province, and in his presence uttered the words which had the power to remove him from local prejudice and personal spite into an atmosphere of impersonal justice: "I appeal unto Caesar." The governor gave the required answer, the only one that could be made: "Thou hast appealed unto Caesar, unto Caesar shalt thou go." And Paul, conducted by Roman soldiers, went to Rome.

When early in the third century all free-born citizens of every city in the empire were given the Roman citizenship, the conception of a universal community, over-riding narrow national bounds, and of a world-peace, the ideal men have always yearned for, seemed on the point of accomplishment.

Undoubtedly the idea was of Greek not Roman origin. It came to Rome by way of Greek philosophy and Alexander the Great, but the Romans alone brought it down to earth and made it work. Law, which is the practical realization of the ideal of justice, was naturally and inevitably first and foremost a Roman product. The Greeks theorized; the Romans translated their theories into action. And it must always be remembered, too, that they and no other nation were the inheritors of the great Greek thought. The town that fought its way to the position of mistress of the western world and a considerable portion of the eastern and southern, too, did not surpass the other peoples of the earth solely in the power to obey better, to fight more intelligently, and to bear hardship with stiffer-backed endurance. Only the Romans really perceived what Greece had been. They admired her often to their own harm; they copied her instead of developing their own natural bent, but they recognized her greatness and they showed thereby their own.

Another certain indication of a nobility in the Roman strain and a lofty ideality, too, which seems strangely remote from the Rome of Cicero and Horace, is given by their golden-deed stories. The stories a nation repeats about its great men show, as nothing does more, the national ideal. Did Nelson really say, "England expects every man to do his duty"? Did Francis I exclaim, "*Tout est perdu fors l'honneur*"? Perhaps they did, but certainly if they had not, some other Englishman, some other Frenchman, would have been found to hang the words upon, so completely do they express the English and the French ideas of the thing to say when a man is up against it. And whether Regulus did in actual truth go back to Carthage to die under torture because he had promised, or not, is unimportant in revealing the Roman character compared with the fact that the story was repeated through the centuries as showing how Romans thought a man should keep his word.

No other nation has tales of heroism and patriotic devotion and disinterested virtue to compare with the Roman: Horatius at the bridge, Curtius leaping into the gulf, the boy threatened with torture to make him reveal the Roman plans, who thrusts his hand into the fire and holds it there—numbers of them have come down, splendid stories, unsurpassed by those of any other people and very rarely equalled. Even if not one of them ever happened they are true, exactly as the accounts of the games are true. They were Roman conceptions and they embodied what Romans believed human beings should and could achieve. The national ideal is an important factor in understanding a nation. High honor and love of country that made nothing of torture and death was what the Romans set first as the greatest thing of all.

As regards Roman literature and art, in the one as in the other all the Romans did for a long time was to try to follow the Greek way, in spite of the fact that it pointed in a direction where their own genius would not naturally have led them. Greek art and Greek letters have little in common with the Roman, although Cicero would have disputed the assertion, and with reason. He had been carefully trained and cultivated in the Greek tradition. Greek art was the whole of art to him; he was not aware of any other. No doubt that lovely ivy-embowered villa of his was done in strict conformity with Greek canons of taste and transplanted to Athens would have seemed perfectly in keeping there. All Roman culture came from Greece, and respectful copies and adaptations of Greek statues and temples and houses were all that Rome wanted. Horace, too, might have disputed the assertion. A Greek could hardly have been more aware than he was of the loveliness of his bit of land, his elms and poplars and smooth lawn sloping to the river. But he, like Cicero, was the foster-child of Greece. The Greek lyric poets were his models and his eye had been trained by them. He saw beauty where they pointed to it, in the ordinary surroundings of life.

That was the peculiar gift of the Greeks, to perceive the beauty of familiar, every-day things, and their art and literature which was concerned to reveal this beauty, is the great example of classic art and literature as distinguished from romantic. The Greeks were the classicists of antiquity and they are still today the pre-eminent classicists. What marked all they did, the classic stamp, is a direct simplicity in expressing the significance of actual life. It was there the Greek artists and poets found what they wanted. The unfamiliar and the extraordinary were on the whole repellent to them and they detested every form of exaggeration. Their desire was to express truthfully what lay at hand, which they saw as beautiful and full of meaning.

But that was not the Roman way. When not directly under Greek guidance the Roman did not perceive beauty in every-day matters, or indeed care to do so. Beauty was unimportant to him. Life in his eyes was a very serious and a very arduous business, and he had no time for what he would have thought of as a mere decoration of it. Before money and leisure had corrupted the nation, as all Romans thought they had, the natural Roman attitude toward art, even the attitude of the best and greatest spirits, was very like what that of the commander of a beleaguered fort would be if he saw one of his men busily carving into a pleasing shape the handle of his weapon. There were imperative tasks to summon men for all that was in them. Painting, sculpture, such-like tri-fles, were to be left to what a Roman writer called "the hungry Greekling."

Still, as Rome grew rich and strong and proud, she felt, of course, the need to display her power by a visible magnificence, and she built splendid temples and palaces and triumphal arches, but they were all Greekish—Greek seen through Roman eyes, bigger and better Greek. To the Roman the big was in itself admirable. The biggest temple in the world was as such better than the rest. If a Corinthian capital was lovely, two, one on top of the other, would be twice as lovely. But at bottom none of all that decorative splendor was Roman, the stately temples that housed Grecian gods, the processions of white-clad priests and vestals winding up the Capitoline with youths and maidens singing a hymn to deities whose home was a Greek island in the Ægean. Such things were all very right and proper to mark the correct grandeur of official Rome, but they had nothing to do with the real religion of a Roman. The worship dear to his heart was given to the little household gods, tiny, rude figures, to which were offered no frankincense, no choice yearling from the flock, nothing rare or precious, but only a bit of the every-day food. We do not hear of any beauty or dignity connected with their worship. That would have estranged the Roman and put him off. Beauty and dignity were appropriate in the imposing temple of Jupiter, Greatest and Best, but for daily use give him comfortable homeliness. The Greeks would have found rude homeliness uncomfortable. They had to have their very pots and pans agreeable to look at.

But when the Romans stopped thinking about culture and the Greeks and devoted themselves to the things they really wanted to do, then they showed that they, too, could create beauty, beauty on a great scale, but always as a by-product, not deliberately sought. "In Rome the true artist is the engineer." Roman genius was called into action by the enormous practical needs of a world empire. Rome met them magnificently. Buildings tremendous, indomitable, amphitheatres where eighty thousand could watch a spectacle, baths where three thousand could bathe at the same time, which nearly two thousand years have left practically intact. Bridges and aqueducts that spanned wide rivers and traversed great spaces with a beautiful, sure precision of soaring arches and massive piers. And always along with them the mighty Roman road, a monument of dogged, unconquerable human effort, huge stone joined to huge stone, marching on and on irresistibly, through unknown hostile forests, over ramparts of mountains, across sunbaked deserts, to the very edges of the habitable world.

That is the true art of Rome, the spontaneous expression of the Roman spirit, its keen realization of the adaptation of practical means to practical ends, its will-power and enduring effort, its tremendous energy and audacity and pride. Beauty was a purely incidental result, not consciously brought about by any thought of it in engineers and builders faced with problems of terrific difficulty, but only by the curious agreement there exists in the nature of things between an admirably utilitarian creation and non-utilitarian beauty.

The conscious art of such a people would be, so any one would reason, sternly realistic, revealing life as pitiless fact, with no desire to express anything except implacable truth. And such is the case with the peculiarly Roman achievement in sculpture, the portrait-bust. These heads are all implacably true with the external truth of accuracy. An exact likeness was all the sculptor sought. He reproduced in his marble every detail of the heads of the hard-faced, tired old men who were to be immortalized, not one unhappy line spared us in the deeply corrugated brow or one fold in the heavy hanging flesh beneath the chin, no least softening of the stupid brutality or the peevish ill-humor which so often dominates the whole. A Roman did not ask to be flattered. He was content with what he was. The more faithful the portrait, the greater the artist's success in the eyes of his patron. This is as true of the women as of the men. An empress did not want her hard mouth softened or the long lobes of her big ears curtailed. A great courtesan complacently allowed the ugly lines of her head and brow to be set down without extenuation. It is impossible to avoid the conviction that they either did not see ugliness, or were indifferent to it. How far removed this photography in marble is from the realism of the Greeks becomes instantly clear if one calls to mind the statue of the Greek girl bending over the basin to wash her hands. Classic art is embodied in her; a commonplace act is invested with perfect beauty.

Now and again among the Roman statues there is one like that of the Chief Vestal, which rises above the exact reproduction of an individual face into a kind of grandeur through the very faithfulness of the transcriber who put with precision into marble the virile force, the profound gravity, the strength without a shadow of human weakness, which made that face a type of what Rome believed herself to be. But these are the rare exceptions.

For the rest, when the Roman sculptors were not copying Greece—and making the copies heavy and ill-proportioned— they took with enthusiasm to allegorical bas-reliefs, the counterpart of Horace's sermons, where the artist sermonized and admiring Rome was edified, *l'art pour la moralité* never more consciously pursued and the art completely over-weighted by the morality. Only in one small department Rome achieved a rich beauty of her own, in those familiar, often-copied panels of the teeming gifts of earth—fruits and flowers and chubby boys gathering great bunches of grapes from weighted vines, shocks of full-eared grain, and cows and sheep, one crowding upon the other almost without design, all the luxuriant abundance poured forth by the copious fertility of the south. They are truly Roman; they have nothing in common with the sparing use in Greek decoration of the flower-pattern. The Greek soil did not lavish her gifts from a never-emptied horn of plenty. Fruits, flowers, like everything else in Greece, were to be used by the artist "with economy."

One of the great Victorians has said that if classicism is the love of the usual in beauty, romanticism is the love of the strange in beauty, and the statement gives to admiration the essence of the difference between the two. The very words romance, romantic, call up a vision, vague yet bright, that banishes the drabness and monotony of every-day life with a sense of possible excitements and adventures. Of course, if every-day life did not look drab and monotonous there would be no reason to turn to romance. That is primarily why the Greeks were not romantic. Facts were full of interest to them. They found enough beauty and delight in them to have no desire to go beyond.

But to the Romans facts were not beautiful nor, in themselves, interesting. The eagerness for inquiry into everything in the universe which had stamped Greece never reached Rome. Cicero's remark that the investigation of nature seeks to find out either things which nobody can know or things which nobody needs to know, expresses perfectly the Roman attitude. They were not an intellectual people. Their place was the world of practical affairs, not of thought. Science ended as Greece went down and Rome came up. Romans travelled all over the earth, but they did not become geographers; they solved the problems of the arch as it had never been done before, but they were not physicists. They were persistently indifferent to theory. It was enough for them to know that such a thing could be accomplished in such a way; the reason was unimportant. They were not interested in why, only in how.

Beauty was still less interesting. It was never quite real to them. Reality, facts, they saw as we do, chiefly as ugly and unpleasant. "Face the facts," "Come down to reality"—the phrases would have had the same meaning to the Romans that they have to us. How hideous and grim reality can be was forced upon their attention as it is not upon ours. We have learned to protect ourselves by shutting away within stone walls shocking sights, but in Rome after the great slave insurrection the main road to the city was lined for more than a mile with the crosses of crucified slaves. Even the horrors of war we disguise in part, but when a friend of Plutarch's visited a battlefield which had established an emperor on the throne, he found bodies piled up sometimes as high as the eaves of a little temple there. In plain, cold fact, reality, as they saw it was more often hateful than not. Their very amusements were perpetually showing them the horrible forms human agony and death can take.

When a people see chiefly ugliness in the world, they will find a refuge from it. Roman literature took the turn which literature has again and again taken when reality is perceived as nothing from which men can get spiritual delight. The writers of Rome's golden age of letters turned to romance.

What we today call realism, the view that life is devoid of beauty and meaning, always has romance for a companion. They do not go hand in hand, but one follows close behind the other, to catch up ever and again and outstrip it for a while and then fall back. The human spirit will not live long at a time in the prison of senseless ugliness. Invariably a romantic reaction comes. The Greeks, who would have nothing to do with extremes, knew neither the one nor the other. They were realists to whom the real was beautiful and the direct expression of that spirit is classic art.

But the Romans, to whom the real was the reverse of beautiful, ended inevitably by turning away from it to romance. Catullus is one of the rare examples of both points of view in one man. He is himself representative of the Roman spirit complete. He sighs to Lesbia from the very height of romantic love; he writes enchanting fairy tales of strange mythological creatures and soars away from everything on earth; then he comes down, to find only filthy mire and to write verses about his factual surroundings which are uglier by far even than the portrait-busts. Reality was in general hideous to him. He had perpetually to escape from it, only to return and then again reject it.

In the Augustan age, the result of a cruel and bitter war which had not brought even to the victors the high exultation of a great enterprise achieved, Roman literature came to its full stature of growth, and the greatest writers of the period turned away from reality and their own world where peace had been bought at the price of republican liberty, to the world of romance and the wonderful regions open to the imagination. The golden age of Roman literature is not classic, but romantic.

XI

Enter the Romantic Roman

Virgil, Livy, Seneca

A great literary gossip of the second century A.D. whose work has come down to us in many volumes and whose name was Aulus Gellius has recorded a comparison he once heard a literary friend of his make between Pindar's and Virgil's description of Ætna in eruption. The Greek poet writes: "In the darkness of the night the red flame whirls rocks with a roar far down to the sea. And high aloft are sent fearful fountains of fire." Virgil says: "Skyward are sent balls of flame that lick the stars and ever and again rocks are spewed forth, the torn entrails of the mountains, and molten crags are hurled groaning to heaven." "Pindar," the critic pointed out to his friend, "describes what actually happened and what he saw with his own eyes, but Virgil's 'balls of flame that lick the stars' is a useless and foolish elaboration, and when he says crags are molten and groan and are hurled to heaven, this is such an account as Pindar never wrote and is monstrous." That is a comparison between a classic and a romantic description. Pindar was using his eyes, Virgil his imagination. The man who compared them was a classicist who, of course, detested romantic exaggeration, and could not see the grandeur that we see in Virgil's "flame that licks the stars."

The romantic artist must not be judged by the canon of strict accuracy. He will not be bound by fact, "the world being inferior to the soul," as Bacon says, "by reason whereof there is a more ample greatness, a more exact goodness, and a more absolute variety, than can be found in the nature of things." To the classicist the nature of things is the truth and he desires only to see clearly what it is. The romanticist is the adventurer drawn on by the new and the strange where to him truth is to be found. The classic writer depends upon reason no less than upon imagination. To the romantic writer imagination can transcend the narrow limits of experience and move on unhampered by it to what eye hath not seen nor ear heard.

The *Æneid* from first to last is pure romance and Virgil, Rome's greatest poet, is one of the world's greatest romanticists.

He was a few years older than Horace who loved him and wrote of him with tender admiration. Everyone seems to have felt like that about him. The allusions to him in Latin literature show a feeling far beyond that for any other man of letters, and in later days it is safe to say that of all poets, of all writers, indeed, he has been the most loved and praised. He was the only ancient author, either Greek or Roman, to make his way into the Christian church. There was a legend, often repeated and embodied in a hymn, that St. Paul had visited his grave and dropped a tear upon it. Again and again his name was introduced into a ritual of the church as one of the prophets, because in an early poem he wrote of a child about to be born who would bring back the golden age and the reign of peace, interpreted by the Christians as meaning the birth of Christ. So all his poems became in some sort sanctified. The monasteries most hostile to pagan learning could allow copies of them, and pious Christians felt it no sin to use him for looking into the future by opening the *Æneid* and reading the first line their eyes happened to light upon. His transformation into a magician was the next step, and as such the polished, suave man of letters figured strangely during the Middle Ages. To Dante he was "the poet," the one to conduct him through Hell and Purgatory, and "my master and my author, he who taught me the good style that did me honor." And from his death on to the present, from Juvenal who—early in the second century— deplored the schoolmaster's hardships in having to listen to "the same daily fare always repeated from the soot-blackened Virgil," up to the last June before the College Board examinations, the generations of school children have owed part of their training to him. In our western world the Bible alone has had a wider influence. From this point of view he is more important than the poets of Greece. For seventeen or eighteen hundred years, he was the master of literature to all the western nations.

The romantic spirit took root and spread through Europe; the classic spirit departed. So much is fact. How far the great Latin romantics were responsible for the change is one of the matters not susceptible of proof. It is impossible to say what would have happened if Virgil and Livy and their greatly inferior, but very influential follower, Seneca, had not lived. In the immense German forests, in the soft sea-airs of Ireland, there were no sharp, clear outlines as in Greece. Luminous mists made dim distances where the imagination was free to see what it chose. Also as the church grew in power, side by side with the intellectualizing effort of dogmatic theology, eastern mysticism worked, with its absolute conviction of "a more ample greatness, a more exact goodness than can be found in the nature of things." There was much apart from Roman literature that pointed to romanticism. But, at the least, it may be said with certainty that Virgil and Livy inaugurated the new movement of the spirit the world was ready for. Classicism had grown thinner and dryer from the beginning of the fourth century B.C. on. It became precious, pedantic, all polished surface. Learning and style were the combination out of which to make poetry. This tendency is the evil genius of the classic spirit and has killed it many a time since the polite and erudite and cultivated society of Alexandria dealt it the blow which by the time Virgil appeared had been fatal to it.

"A talent is formed in stillness," said Goethe, "a character in the stream of the world." That is the romantic view; the Greeks of the great age would have violently disagreed. The stream of the world was to them precisely the place to develop the artist, the classical artist, whose eyes are ever turned upon life. But it is not the place to develop the imagination. The romantic artist with-draws from the busy haunts of men to some fair and tranquil retreat, in Sicilian meadows, or by the deep blue sea of the south, or on the hillslope of an English lake, where he may see and tell of things invisible to mortal sight. Alone of the Augustan poets Virgil had no love for life in Rome. During all the years that he wrote he lived in the country, near the Bay of Naples. Even Augustus, who cared much for him and recognized early his genius, was unable to persuade him to do more than make brief visits to the capital.

Very little is known about him. His home was near Mantua and he lost it as Horace did his after the republican cause was defeated. In Naples they called him "the maiden," for his purity of life, some said, others, for his gentleness, and it may be both had a share in the nickname. He went once to Greece and Horace wrote a poem to the ship that carried so precious a burden. One account is that he died on the way home, another, that this hap-pened after a second voyage. Our gossip, Aulus Gellius, tells at length how on his death bed he begged his friends to burn the *Æneid*, "because," Gellius says, "those parts which he left per-fected and polished enjoy the highest praise for poetical beauty, but those which he was unable to revise because he was overtaken by death are not worthy of the taste of the most elegant of poets." Augustus is said to have prevented this last wish from being ful-filled. The point of the story is, of course, the intense desire it shows on Virgil's part for perfected finish, and this is borne out by the length of time he spent on each piece of writing—eleven years given to the *Æneid* alone.

Before he began it he had written two poems or sets of poems: the earlier his *Eclogues*—in English, *Selections*—which were an imitation of a Sicilian poet's pastoral verse, but oddly Romanized, so that the shepherds every now and then stop singing of flocks and herds and flowery meadows and the lovely Galatea, to discuss political doings and burst forth into Caesar's praises; the later, his *Georgics*—a Greek word meaning the tillage of the land—a unique and very beautiful poem, the literary equivalent of the lovely fruit and flower panel. "What makes a cornfield smile; under what star the soil should be upturned and when it suits best for wedding the vine to the elm; what care oxen need; what is the method of breeding cattle; and what is the weight of men's experience in preserving the frugal commonwealth of bees; such is the song I now essay." So the poem begins. It is practical husbandry done in lovely verse, an achievement which would off-hand appear impossible, and has certainly never been repeated since. There are careful descriptions of the soil each crop needs, the time for planting and watering and weeding; a long description of how to breed the farm animals, together with a detailed account of the diseases they are liable to and their remedies; and lastly, everything conceivable about bee-culture, including the fact, even to Virgil mildly surprising, that they do not bring forth their young as do all other creatures, but "pick them up in their mouths from leaves and grateful herbage."

The good, common-sense directions are exquisitely decorated: "The best planting season for vines is the bloom of spring, spring that does good to woodland foliage and forestry. It is then that the pathless brakes are musical with singing birds and the cattle pair in their season. The fostering soil brings forth, and the warm western winds unseal the womb of the fields. A gentle moisture rises over all and the young vine branch puts out its buds and unfolds all its leaves. I do not believe the days were fairer or their course more blissful when the young world first came into being; it was spring then—it was spring-tide that the great globe was keeping, when an iron race of men rose from the hard soil and beasts were turned into the woods and stars into the sky."

But a quotation here and there can show nothing really of what the poem is. The slow course of the narrative, the piling up of detail after detail in the life of the farm, the deep feeling for earth and her produce, the sense of the primal value of the labor that causes earth to produce, end by making a powerful impression of the beauty and the meaning in these fundamentals of human life.

It is the poem in which Virgil and Latin poetry come nearest to the classic.

Now and again, however, the Roman gets the better of the artist. Virgil sees no reason why cattle disease is not a subject for a poet, and he tells at length about "the noisome scab" on sheep, and how to open with a knife "the mouth of the swollen sore," and about "the panting cough that shakes diseased swine," when "black blood trickles from their nostrils," and the dying agonies of a bull stricken with distemper, "convulsed and vomiting bloody foam"—a veterinary's pamphlet sonorously versified.

The note of exaggeration, too, foreign to classic art and always at home in romantic art, is never far away: "The bull comes upon his foe like a billow that begins to grow white out in midsea, curving up like a bellying sail—like it also when it rolls to shore and roars terrific among the rocks, breaking high as the towering cliff." And at the very end the poem lapses into wild romanticism; the poet wanders away from his bees to the bottom of the ocean and all manner of fantastic creatures of the sea with "grass-green glare of fiery eyes." Virgil was at last trying his hand at mythology. From this ending to the subject of the *Æneid* there was but a short step.

A romantic subject may be treated classically and a classic subject romantically. The beauty of a Greek god is human, realized by the artist from the living men he had seen; it is what a romantic subject will become under classic treatment. The romance has suffered: the statue is a god merely because it is so labelled. The strange beauty of a Hindoo god, like nothing ever seen on earth, is completely romantic. The Hindoo artist's imagination has conceived something beyond or, at the least, apart from, humanity. The same distinction emerges from a comparison between the romantic *Æneid* and the classic *Iliad*. The *Iliad* has as romantic a subject as the *Æneid*, as romantic, indeed, as there could be: battles where heroes and gods fight for a marvellously beautiful woman, and conclaves held in silver Olympus where deities watch the contest and give victory to this side or that. But when Homer's method of treatment is compared with Virgil's the difference between classic romanticism and the purely romantic is instantly perceived.

In the *Iliad*, Achilles has lost his armor, and his goddess-mother goes to the fire-god to beg a new set from him. She finds him "in his halls wrought of brass by his own hand, sweating and toiling and with busy hand plying the bellows. He was fashioning a score of tripods, all placed on wheels of gold that they might roll in and back, a marvel to behold. Not yet was added the neat handles, for which the god was forging rivets busily." This description of a god, like the Greek statue, is a classic treatment of a romantic theme which does damage to the romance. The classic artist's home is the earth; if he ascends to heaven, heaven takes on the look of earth. But when Æneas loses his armor and his mother goes to Vulcan for the same purpose there is nothing of earth in the scene: "An island towering with fiery mountains; beneath thunders a cavern blasted out by the Cyclops' forges; the sound of mighty blows echo on anvils; molten metal hisses; fires dart from the great jaws of the furnace. Hither the lord of fire descends from heaven's height. There in the mighty cave the Cyclops were forging"—not smoothly rolling tripods fitted with neat handles, but "the thunderbolt, one of those many which the great Father showers down on earth. Three spokes of frozen rain, three of watery cloud, had they put together, three of ruddy flame and the winged wind of the south; and now they blend the awful flash and the noise and the terror and the fury of the untiring lightning flame." That is what your true romantic can do with the fearful fire-god and the forges of the Cyclops. Thunderbolts, every reader must feel, are what ought to be produced by such means.

If it is objected that the pictures of the supernatural in the *Iliad* are not classic, but only primitive, the truth is that the realism so strikingly marked in Homer is essentially the same as that which stamps the whole of Greek art. It is not a mere matter of childish details. His Olympians are human just as the Hermes and the Venus of Milo are.

When the Old Testament writer says that the Lord God was walking in the garden in the cool of the evening, he too, like Homer, is doing all that a classicist can do with such a subject: he makes it delightful, quaint and charming. But the description in the Book of Revelation, "And I saw a great white throne and him that sat on it, from whose face the earth and the heaven fled away and there was found no place for them," is the work of a lofty romantic imagination.

To us romance means chiefly the passion of love. The Greeks, Plato excepted, did not think much of that as a subject for literature. They practically ignored it. Even Greek tragedy has very little to do with it. The romantic lover, we know, is allied to the lunatic, and the Greeks had a complete prepossession in favor of sanity. To be sure, the *Iliad* centres in Helen, but Homer's treatment of the loveliest woman of the world is soberly matter-of-fact. When Paris is about to be killed by Menelaus, Aphrodite saves him and carries him away to Troy and his own house. Then she goes to find Helen and bring her to him. Helen is sullen and unwilling. She bids the goddess if she loves him so much, to serve him herself, "and he may take thee for his wife—or his handmaid. I will never go to share his couch." But under Aphrodite's threats she does go and speaks to Paris scornfully, with averted eyes: "Thou hast left the battle. Would thou hadst perished by the mighty hand of him who was my husband. Once thou didst boast to be his peer. Then up—defy him. Yet I counsel thee not—for fear he smite thee and thou be slain." Paris takes all this with the serenity of a man who knows he is going to have what he wants no matter how his wife talks. Menelaus is victor at the moment, he tells her, but he may yet vanquish him in turn. "But now is the time for love. Never before have I felt such sweetness of desire. He spake and went to his fair couch and the lady followed him." There could be nothing less romantic. Angry, scolding, reluctant Helen, and Paris completely indifferent to all save one thing.

Virgil could do a great love story. Æneas and Dido are not only the hero and heroine of our very first romance, they are great lovers, too, the woman the greater, as through the ages the poets have loved to portray her. She "is pierced by love's cruel shaft, feeding the wound with her life-blood and wasting under a hidden fire"; if she is with him "she begins to speak and stops midway in the utterance"; he speaks and "she hangs upon his lips." When the night comes and the banquet hall is empty, she steals there from her bed to find the couch he had lain on and stretch herself upon it. "Him far away she sees and hears, herself far away."

The episode of the hunting party is ushered in with all the trappings of romance. Before the palace door "Dido's charger splendid in purple and gold champs his foaming bit." The queen "comes forth with a great company attending her. Her cloak was purple bordered with embroidery; her quiver of gold, her hair knotted up with gold, her purple dress was fastened with a golden clasp." A hero's beauty in romance is quite as important as a heroine's, and when Æneas joins her he is "like Apollo as he leaves his wintry Lycia and visits Delos, his mother-isle; his flowing hair restrained by a wreath of soft leaves and entwined with gold; his arrows ring upon his shoulders. Even so swift came Æneas, such the beauty that shone forth from his peerless look and mien." Their union, when the hunt is broken up by the storm, takes place in surroundings perfectly fitted to two such personages, a Gustave Doré cavern lit by lightning flashes and echoing the roll of thunder and the cry of the mountain nymphs.

Virgil's attitude at this point in the story, the Roman attitude, was to have a far-reaching influence. Dido has made the fatal slip; her good name is lost; she has fallen from her high estate. Not so

Æneas; the matter is merely incidental to him. His good name is not affected at all. Jupiter sends down the messenger god to bid him remember his high charge to found the Roman race, and he makes ready to sail with little more distress than at the difficulty of how to break the news to her: "What first beginning can he make?" But for her, of course, everything is over. She pleads with him for a moment in beautiful, tender words: "Flying, and from me? By these tears and by your plighted hand—since I myself have left my wretched self nothing else to plead—by our union, by marriage-rites yet unfulfilled, if in anything I have deserved well of you, if anything of mine was ever sweet to you"—but the gods have spoken and Æneas must go, and all that is left for Dido and her tarnished fair fame is death, the only refuge in such straits for the romantic heroine through all the centuries since.

Here is a great change from Homer and his treatment of Helen. A long way has been travelled on the long road of woman's destiny. In the *Iliad*, Helen is not blamed at all. What could a woman do but go with whatever man was at hand to carry her off? All the blame is put upon Paris. In the *Odyssey*, when Telemachus goes to Menelaus' palace to ask news of his father, Helen comes down into the great hall, lovely and serene. A handmaid places a well-wrought chair for her; another brings her silver work-basket, and Helen sits and works and talks tranquilly of ruined Troy and the men gaze adoringly. Homer is logical: a woman was helpless in those days; the fault could not be hers. But Roman women were not like that ever; they were responsible human beings, a force to be reckoned with; Dido clearly did not have to yield to Æneas. Then, by a curious shifting of the balance, all the blame was put upon her. Æneas got none of it. This was the Roman point of view, in line with all the early stories of Lucretia and Virginia and the like, and embodied in Virgil's poem it went over the whole western world, never even challenged until almost the end of the nineteenth century. Trollope held it as firmly as Virgil. When lovely woman stooped to folly, her only refuge was to die,

while the man in the case did just as Æneas did, married somebody else.

The completely romantic view of woman, as what Havelock
Ellis called "a silly angel," is only dimly foreshadowed by Virgil.
It could never have found a real footing in Rome. Dido is the
Roman matron, remembering for her consolation as she dies that
she has built a splendid city and avenged a brother's death. But
the foundation for the later development was laid, and the long
line of lovely, innocent, trusting women, betrayed to their undo-
ing, who for hundreds of years took possession of romance, goes
directly back to the *Æneid*.

There is nothing more romantic than heroism and great deeds
in battle and a glorious death. They are all ideas Greek literature
fights shy of. The *Iliad* is a poem of battles but there is very little
talk about glory of any kind, and none at all about the glory of a
noble death. Homer's heroes all know that there is a time for heroism and a time not. When a mightier warrior faces them they
retreat, even if unwillingly, "for this sore grief enters my heart,
Hector some day shall boast that I fled before his face," but they
never lose the common-sense point of view that "there is no
shame in fleeing from ruin, yea, even in the night. Better he fares
who flees from trouble than he that is overtaken." A matter-of-
fact atmosphere pervades the ringing plains of windy Troy. When
Ajax dares to fight with Hector and withstand him, his reward at
close of day is substantial: "And wide-ruling Agamemnon gave to
Ajax slices of the full length of the [roasted] ox's back for his
honor." Homeric heroes do a great deal of eating and drinking and
cooking, too; there are receipts given, how to make a pleasant
drink from grated cheese and wine and barley, what relishes go
best with wine, and so on. The things of daily life play quite as
prominent a part as valorous deeds do and "the joy of battle."

All this is completely unlike the *Æneid*. The heroes there are
not human beings, but bigger, stronger, grander. Hector in the
Iliad advancing to battle is "like a stalled horse, full fed at the

manger, when he breaks his tether and speeds exultingly over the plain," or—the extreme of romantic description in the poem—"all in bronze shone Hector even as the lightning of Father Zeus." But Æneas in the same case is "vast as Mount Athos or Mount Eryx, vast as Father Apennine himself when he shakes his mighty oaks and lifts his snow-topped peak to the sky," or "like Ægaeon who, fable tells, had a hundred arms and a hundred hands and flashed fire through fifty mouths from the depths of fifty bosoms, thundering on fifty strong shields and drawing fifty sharp swords— even so Æneas slakes his victorious fury the whole field over."

No one in the *Æneid*, except Dido alone, ever comes down to earth. The heroes never are afraid. They fight for glory only and in its pursuit they are as disdainful of death as the knights of the Round Table or Charlemagne's paladins. "The combatants rush on glorious death through a storm of wounds" over and over again. They pray for death and they go willingly to meet it. "Death I fear not," a wounded warrior cries advancing upon Æneas, "I come to die." "Have compassion upon me," another hero, defeated, prays. "Dash me on reef, on rock, that none may know my shame." Æneas bitterly regrets that he did not die when Troy fell:

> Ye Troyan ashes and dear shades of mine,
> I call you witness, that at your last fall
> I fled no stroke of any Greekish sword,
> And if the fates would I had fallen in fight,
> That by my hand I did deserve it well.

But Homer's heroes never want to die. Death is the worst of ills. "Then Hector knew the truth in his heart and he spoke and said, Aye, now verily is evil death come very nigh me nor is there way of escape. He ended and the dark shadow of death came down and his soul flew forth and was gone to the house of Hades, wailing his fate, leaving fair youth and vigor."

Nowhere, indeed, is the distinction between the classicist and the romanticist seen more clearly than in the way they regard death. On the whole, in Latin literature death is desirable. Even to Horace, the most classic in spirit of all Roman writers, it is "sweet and seemly to die for one's country." English poetry has the same tendency in a notable degree, "Eloquent, just and mighty death," "Dear, beauteous death, the jewel of the just"—there are endless examples. It is the romantic view: the lure to the spirit of the mystery life cannot solve, the sense of all that the unknown may hold, the thrill of the final great adventure. But to the classicist death is always evil unalloyed. Homer's heroes speak in that respect for all Greece. His familiar line that it is better to be a serf on earth than to rule over the dead gives the Greek point of view.

Quotations to decorate soldiers' monuments are found by the score in Latin, but not in Greek. Greek heroism wears an air of soberness always. It is never exultant. The epitaphs the Greeks set on their own soldiers' monuments do not praise heroic death or speak of glory. In all their literature they talk very little of either. They saw too clearly the agony they are rooted in. The Roman boy's thrusting his hand into the fire was beyond question magnificent, a superb gesture of defiance, but I believe a Greek would have been hard put to it to understand it. The Greeks had no gestures. Æneas, when the great storm comes upon him, lifts his hands to heaven and cries aloud, "Oh, thrice and four times blessed, those who died beneath the walls of Troy." The words are taken from the *Odyssey*, but spoken so differently. Odysseus huddled in the bottom of the boat says them wretchedly to himself. It is impossible to imagine the Greek hero declaiming them to the winds and waves, but it is completely in keeping with the Latin. All the talk in the *Æneid* is grand. To Virgil, the romantic, the ordinary had no place in an epic. But the classic Homer thought otherwise.

The real subject of the *Æneid* is not Æneas, as the real subject of the *Iliad* is the wrath of Achilles; it is Rome and the glories of her empire, seen as the romanticist sees the great past. The first title given it was *The Deeds of the Roman People*. Æneas is important because he carries Rome's destiny; he is to be her founder by the high decrees of fate. Repeatedly in the poem the names of the men who made Rome are rehearsed, glowing history in noble poetry: "Love of country shall conquer and the unmeasured thirst for glory. Look—the Decii and the Drusi and Torquatus with his pitiless ax, and Camillus bringing home the standards saved. What tongue would leave you unpraised, great Cato, or you, great Cossus, or pass over in silence the race of the Gracchi or the two Scipios, twin thunderbolts of war, Africa's ruin, or Fabricius mighty in his poverty, or you, Serranus, sowing your own ploughed field? Others, I doubt not, will mold better the breathing bronze to life-like softness and from marble draw forth living faces. They will plead better at the bar, and mark out the courses of the sky with their rod and tell of the rising stars. Do you, Roman, remember to rule nations with power supreme. Your art shall be this, to impose the custom of peace, to spare the humbled and war down the proud."

The words are a poetical condensation of Livy's history. No connection or acquaintance, even, between the two men is mentioned anywhere, but the connection between their work is close. Livy was considerably the younger, but he had been engaged upon his history for some ten or twelve years before Virgil died. The two must have known each other's work. Livy's idea of "the founding of this great city and the establishment of an empire which is now in power next to the immortal gods" is precisely Virgil's. Both men took the same theme and the prose writer saw it almost as romantically as the poet: Rome was built up by men of grand character, who were the instruments of divine providence and who were governed by a standard of simple goodness unknown to the corruptions of civilization.

Through Livy's pages moves a solemn pageant of stately figures, all the heroes, the soldiers, statesmen, patriots, who for Rome's sake endured to die and are immortal for ever. That classic sense for fact which so drove on Polybius, Terence's friend, the Greek historian, that he must travel over the Alps, a terrific journey then, to test the accounts of Hannibal's passage before writing about it, that sent him hurrying here and there to read an old inscription or an ancient book, never troubled Livy at all. He was sure of the only ground he really cared about, that "Romans never were worsted in an open fight or upon equal terms," that every war Rome fought was "just and pious," and that all of Rome's enemies were base and treacherous. His simple course when authorities differed was to choose the account most favorable to Rome. As a historian he must yield to the Greek, but he has been a living influence through the centuries since he wrote, while Polybius, so accurate and so dull, has not lived at all outside the scholar's library. Polybius' account of Hannibal is painstakingly careful and completely unimpressive. The Hannibal we know, the brilliant genius of war, the indomitable master of the Alps, the scourge of Italy, is Livy's creation, as is too the picture of the magnificent tenacity and endurance which finally defeated him.

Livy is a great writer, endowed with the fire and the power of a great imagination. It must not be supposed that he let himself be carried away to invent on occasion. He was a conscientious man who wanted to write only what was true. In his preface he says: "Such things as are reported either before or at the founding of the city, set out more by poet's fables than grounded upon pure and faithful records, I mean neither to assert nor disprove." There was no defect in his honesty, but only in his criticism, and artists are seldom critics.

Goethe's sweeping statement about English writers, that inspiration is everything to them, reflection nothing, is exactly applicable to Livy. He saw only the actors on history's stage; the causes responsible for the drama and what went on behind the scenes meant nothing to him. His real interest was in the good and the great of mankind—of Roman mankind. He had that delightful characteristic, so often a companion to the romantic temperament, enthusiasm. The characters in his history live because he was himself so fired by what they did and suffered. Yet he never lost his grasp on the essential truths of human nature; he had in a high degree imaginative insight. And just as he was able to put himself in the place of one of his great Romans and understand him with an unerring perception, in the same way, through his passionate love for what he saw in that early Rome of republican simplicity and hardihood and self-sacrificing patriotism, and through his sure grasp of the combination of great qualities that was truly Roman, unlike any before or since, he was able to produce a characterization of a nation which lives as much as any of literature's foremost characters live. Rome to us is Livy's Rome.

His place is hardly among historians, as we understand the term. He was more than that. What he wrote has an interest altogether independent of its accuracy. He was a great romantic historian—if the term may be allowed. Like Virgil he showed romance at its best, presenting an ideal which is not supernatural or superhuman, but felt instantly to be realizable, although never yet realized, and which has aroused in unnumbered readers the longing to bring it to pass.

But just as there always follows close upon classicism the danger of an arid superficiality, a pedantry that seeks only correctness and dispenses with life, losing the spirit in the passion for the fact, so romanticism has an evil attending genius, sentimentality. The boundary between the two is so tenuous, so easily overpassed. Virgil transgressed it more than once. The romantic is imaginative, the sentimental is unreal; the romantic is idealistic, the sentimental is false. The mark of insincerity is upon all the sentimental: sentimentality is unconscious insincerity. The romanticist, as such, is as sincere as the classicist; it is only that his idea of truth is different. But the sentimentalist does not care about truth. He is always able to believe what he wants to believe.

Sentimental romance came to Rome very shortly after Livy and Virgil died, and took possession of a field which has ever since been peculiarly open to it, the drama. It was almost inevitable that the sentimental play should be a Roman product. There is a kinship between exaggeration and sentimentality. The sentimental always inclines to the exaggerated, and the Romans with their strong natural leaning toward exaggeration were peculiarly liable to it. In sentimental romance anything is admissible. The writer's only object is to say what his audience want to hear in a way that will hold their interest. And as regards the latter, his field of choice is wide: bent as he is only on what is agreeable, he has no need to trouble himself with considerations of what is natural and probable. Forms of sentimentality vary in different ages and in different countries, but their common source is always easy to see. The Roman variety, of course, insisted upon human nature's being grand and heroic; dauntless courage and unshaken fortitude were the qualities all the sympathetic characters in their romance must possess. It is safe to say that the notion of lovely helplessness would never have had a real development in ancient Rome even if she had lasted centuries longer than she did. But on the whole the general range of sentimental ideas was much what it is today. The popular hero and heroine everywhere show their Roman descent by always regarding death as a negligible matter. To the Roman sentimentalist, exactly as to the modern, every man went joyfully to die for his country and every mother wanted to send her son for the same purpose. The poor and lowly were happier than the rich and powerful; the old farm of boyhood's days to be preferred to marble halls; a mother always a mother, and so on.

All this is completely opposed to what the Greeks wanted. A Greek tragic drama has always, indeed, a romantic subject. The central idea of tragedy is rooted in strangeness, great souls suffering extraordinary calamities, but to the Greek it must be presented classically, which is to say, in the way most opposed to the sentimental, nothing exaggerated, nothing distorted away from nature. A Greek tragedy has no popular appeal, as we understand the words. It is the product of an art austere, reserved, precise to

the verge of hardness; tragedy achieved in the manner most difficult for that achievement, with strict economy of adjective,
description, detail. It had no popular appeal, as the Romans
understood the words, either. The idea of rewriting it to suit
modern Roman taste occurred to a very able man shortly after Virgil died and he became thereby the father of the sentimental
drama.

His name was Seneca and he is best known as a statesman who
for a few years held the reins in Rome, and as a devoted preacher
of the Stoic doctrine. But his influence upon the theatre is his
most enduring title to fame. Along with his Stoicism he had an
ardent romanticism. He set himself to make Greek plays over into
romantic dramas that should give Roman audiences what they
wanted, and to read him is like turning a magnifying glass on
romance and on Rome.

Perhaps the most striking example of what resulted is his *Trojan Women*, based on Euripides' tragedy. A comparison between the
two illustrates clearly the methods of the sentimental romantic.

In both plays the curtain rises upon the battlefield some days
after Troy has fallen. Euripides shows an old woman asleep on the
ground in front. As the day brightens she wakes slowly and lifts
herself up painfully. She talks to herself in words that could be
spoken only quietly, almost dully, as an old woman brought to the
utmost of misery would speak:

> Up from the earth, O weary head.
> This is not Troy, about, above—
> Not Troy, nor we the lords thereof.
> Thou breaking neck, be strengthened.
> . . . .
> Who am I that I sit
> Here at a Greek king's door—
> A woman that hath no home,
> Weeping alone for her dead—

The whole speech is purely human; there is nothing in it of what we call a queenly spirit. To Seneca it seemed very poor, unworthy of royalty and sure to put a Roman audience completely off. His Hecuba is discovered erect with flashing eyes; her queenly spirit is visible in every inch of her, and her speech is delivered to the universe:

> Whoever puts his faith in royal power,
> Who rules in a great hall and trusts to riches,
> Let him behold you, Troy, and look on me.
> Never has fortune shown a greater proof
> How frail is the dependence of the proud.
> Now breaks and falls the lofty pillar—Mighty Asia falls.
> Divinities, hostile to me and mine,
> I call you witness, and I call you too,
> Great sons, my children: bear me witness that
> I, Hecuba, saw all the woe to come.
> I saw it first nor did I fear to speak.
> I told you—

The speech is all like that, with never a touch of pitifulness or human weakness. This Hecuba is not a suffering woman; she is the great queen whose courage no calamity can break. She is also the authoritative and weighty Roman matron as she was popularly conceived, ready to speak her mind on any subject and always able to say, I told you so. Of course she is completely disdainful of death. "Mourn not that Priam has died," she and the Trojan women tell each other. "Dead he is happy, as are all who die in battle." Euripides' Hecuba says:

> Death cannot be what life is, Child. The cup
> Of death is empty and life hath always hope.

She is not heroic. When she hears that the Greek chiefs have drawn lots for her and her companions, and that she has fallen to one of Troy's bitterest foes, she only mourns:

> Weep for me.
> Mine is the crown of misery.

But Seneca's Hecuba hears exultingly that not a man in the host is willing to draw for her—a disposition quite comprehensible to the reader—and cries:

> They fear me! I alone make Greeks afraid.

The climax of each play is the death of Andromache's little son who must be killed in order that Hector's race shall end. In Euripides a very human herald comes to get the boy, who speaks gently to the mother in her agony:

> 'Tis ordered that this child—Oh,
> How can I tell her of it? 'Tis their will
> Thy son shall die. . . . Nay, let the thing
> Be done. Thou shalt be wiser so. Nor cling
> So fiercely to him—

Such a herald of the host would not have impressed a Roman audience, and Seneca himself no doubt thought the speech a very tame prelude to the death of mighty Hector's son. His herald enters, as he declares with his first words, terrified to the depths of his being, a horrid tremor shaking his limbs. As well it might, for he has seen—"I saw it, I myself"—the sun eclipsed and a fearful earthquake that convulsed the sea and sent cliffs crashing down and laid forests low and tore the land apart and opened a fearful cavern from which there breathed a breath as from the dead—to usher forth the ghost of Achilles.

Euripides uses Andromache's farewell to the child to give a picture of suffering as moving as any ever painted:

> Go, die, my best beloved, my cherished one,
> In fierce men's hands, leaving me here alone. . . .
>   Weepest thou?
> Nay, why, my little one? Thou canst not know. . . .
>   Thou little thing
> That curlest in my arms, what sweet scents cling
> All round thy neck. . . . Kiss me. This one time.
> Not ever again—

Seneca did not like that. The Greek poet brought the great mythical figure of the Trojan princess down to earth and made her feel only what any woman in agony might feel. A Roman audience expected something better from Hector's wife. Seneca's Andromache is the Mother, in the grandest aspect of that character known to the stage. She tells the Trojan women that she would of course have killed herself as soon as Hector died except for her child:

> He held me back. 'Tis he who masters me.
> 'Tis he forbids me to seek death.
> . . . Ah, he has taken from me
> The great reward that greatest evils bring,
> To be afraid of nothing.

She then decides to hide him and tell the Greeks that he is dead, but he, in accordance with the best traditions of the Roman boy, refuses with a proud gesture to stoop to such an act. She is joyful at this proof of proper spirit: "You scorn a safe hiding place," she cries, "I know your noble nature." His reluctance is but just overcome and he hidden, when Ulysses comes to get him and instantly suspects a trick. He threatens Andromache with torture, described in detail, if she will not give him up. She, of course, is utterly unmoved. Mothers, she tells him, are never afraid for themselves. Even when the child is finally discovered she keeps her haughty composure; she bids her son be glad, because their reason for killing him is that they are afraid of him: "You are a little boy, indeed, but already one to be feared."

In Euripides' play, when the herald returns he is bringing back the dead child to his mother, but she has gone, a captive in a Greek ship to her son's murderers. The grandmother receives the little dead body and speaks quietly to it:

> Poor little child.
> Was it our ancient wall so savagely hath rent
> Thy curls . . . here where thy mother laid
> Her kisses. Where the bone-edge frayed
> Grins white above—ah, heaven, I will not see. . . .
> Oh, dear proud lips, so full of hope,
> And closed forever—

Then she and the women wrap the body "in linen white," and it is borne off to be buried "in his low sepulchre." The horrors of the death are not mentioned except for that brief speech of Hecuba's.

Seneca's messenger does not bring the dead body back, because as he explains in detail, the height from which the boy was thrown was so great, there was really nothing left except bits ground deep into the earth. However, he tells the mother she must be proud, for the boy endured to die with a great spirit. He walked to his place of death with steps that never faltered. When he reached the summit he looked upon the Greek host fearlessly and they all wept, Ulysses, too. Not an eye dry except the noble boy's. Then pushing away the hands that held him he leaped of his own accord and died, dashed into pieces. "Just like his father," says Andromache, and Hecuba ends the play with the conclusion that death alone is to be desired.

If literature is made up of the best, Seneca is unimportant for Latin literature, but the kind of drama he was the first to write has kept its popularity unimpaired down to today, and if great influence makes a great literary figure, he stands close to the first rank. In his plays the tendencies of Roman thought and feeling stand out in a form so heightened that they are unmistakable. He marks without the possibility of confusion the broad outlines of the Roman way as distinguished from the Greek way, and he is another proof that we are the inheritors not of Greece, but of Rome.

XII

Juvenal's Rome and the Stoics

A strange page of history opens with the death of Augustus, strange and difficult to understand. In less than two centuries after he died Latin literature was practically over and the empire was beginning to fall. The Augustan age, when men of genius wrote books which nearly two thousand years of life assure us are immortal, was the prelude to a swift deterioration and the complete extinction of Roman letters. Four great and good emperors succeeded each other in the second century, giving Europe, the historians declare, a peace and prosperity she was not to see again, and yet during that century the mighty structure of the empire began to collapse. The last of the four, Marcus Aurelius, was a devoted follower of Rome's noble philosophy, Stoicism. He raised it to the throne and through his virtues it acquired a new greatness and a fresh lustre, but with his death it ended. From then on, in the literature that has come down to us, Stoicism is never spoken of as an influence. The history of the first two centuries of the empire is a record of a great literature that ushers in its own destruction, great rulers that leave the Roman state tottering, a great spiritual movement that dies with its highest expression.

No one can doubt that the three are connected. The same causes must lie back of them all, and the final cause must be the weakening and the failure of what the whole world in the last analysis depends on: men's energy and fortitude, their morality and vision. That was certainly taking place during these disastrous years, but the accounts given by contemporary writers show such an extraordinary divergence, it is impossible to bring what they say into a coherent whole or to see cause and effect in any clear detail.

During the two centuries when ancient Rome was dying and Latin literature almost dead, three names stand out: Tacitus the historian, a man of genius hardly surpassed by earlier writers; Juvenal the brilliant and bitter satirist; and Seneca of the sentimental plays, who has left us the best exposition there is in Latin of the Stoic doctrine. His two great successors, Epictetus and Marcus Aurelius, chose to express themselves in Greek and so are technically outside of Roman letters, but they are equally important with Seneca in showing what Stoicism became when it passed from Greece to Rome. The clear picture given by these three last and most famous Stoics of what resulted when a second-rate Greek philosophy had developed into a first-rate Roman religion, together with the history of Tacitus and the satires of Juvenal, are our best sources of knowledge for the momentous years that brought classical antiquity to an end.

But they are not sources consistent with each other. Juvenal's and Tacitus' Rome is so different from that of the Stoics, there is no way to make one city out of the two. Roman life as the historian and the satirist see it is evil without a single mitigating feature. As the Stoics show it, it is lived on loftiest heights with never a descent from them. To Juvenal, private life in Rome was given over to abominable vice; to Tacitus, public life was a mad reign of terror. In Seneca's letters, in the discourses of Epictetus, in Marcus Aurelius' diary, there is an atmosphere of purity, goodness, noble strength, such as pervades few books in all the literature of the world. In this last age of ancient Rome, extremes the most acute existed side by side. No reaction from the one ushered in the other: the spirit of black hopelessness for mankind as sunk irretrievably in the abyss of degradation, stood face to face with the spirit of unshakable confidence in man's divinity.

The picture Tacitus and Juvenal drew is the one the world has accepted. It is so vividly and so powerfully done, the detail so convincing, the colors so sombre and yet so arresting, the impression it makes is overwhelming. All records of infamy seem to pale by comparison. And, at the same time, the sincerity of both writers is instantly apparent; monstrous as the deeds are they relate, the reader never doubts that they took place essentially as they are described. For truth, however, more is needed than sincerity joined to accuracy. Before either comes disinterestedness. The power to disengage oneself from one's subject and put personal bias aside is the first requisite, and this neither the historian nor the satirist, great as they were, possessed. The tasks they set themselves, Juvenal to denounce the age he lived in, Tacitus to write the history of it, were those that need especially a balanced judgment, and both men had come too close personally to the evils of their times to be able to keep the balance. Each was unfortunate in his life, although for completely different reasons, and suffering had warped their point of view before ever they began to write.

Of Juvenal's life nothing is directly known except that it fell during the last part of the first and the early part of the second century. He never writes about himself. Nevertheless no one who reads the satires can doubt that he was a very poor and a very proud man, wretched at living in a city where to be poor was to be perpetually affronted and treated with insolence, often by inferiors, even by slaves. Juvenal's patron was no Maecenas. All he did for his dependents was to ask them occasionally to dinner where they were served different food from that placed before him. He feasted on lobster and asparagus, a mullet from Corsica, a lamprey from Sicily, a fattened goose's liver, a huge capon, a boar with truffles, a peacock—"Gods! a whole boar! entire!—Go, gorged with peacock." The hungry clients got a tiny crab, an eel caught in the sewers, a dubious kind of fungus. "Surely," they whisper, "he will give us what is left of the hare—some scraps of the boar's haunch." But no. "If you can endure this," Juvenal storms, "you deserve it. You will submit to being whipped." And one sees the man of genius stalking home to his attic, his heart burning within him, to stay there until actual starvation drives him to the rich man's door again.

In one passage he describes a school-master's lot in such a way, one cannot but suspect that personal experience is behind the words. "Do you teach? Bowels of iron is what a teacher needs when each pupil stands up in turn and recites the self-same things in the self-same way. The same daily fare again and again—it's death to the wretched master. 'What would I not give,' cries he, 'that the boy's father might listen to him as often as I do.' And you live in a hole no blacksmith would put up with—and the lamps stink—and the boys thumb their begrimed Horace and their smoke-blackened Virgil—Be sure, O parents, to require the teacher to mould the young minds as a man moulds wax—and when the year ends reward him with a jockey's wage."

Such a man condemned to such a life, a genius, acutely sensitive, feeling his degradation at every turn, despising himself for accepting scraps flung him by men he despised, could hardly have failed to see life as a black and desperate business. "If nature denies me talent," he cries, "my indignation will write my verses for me."

Taken by himself alone, if his authority were accepted without question, he would explain clearly, completely, and convincingly why Rome fell. His Rome is inhabited by a vile, degenerate people; it is a place where virtue has all but perished and what little is left exists only to suffer. It is a nightmare city where men must "dread poison when wine sparkles in a golden cup," and wives "learned in the arch-poisoner's arts carry to burial their husbands' blackened corpses," and every day in the year you meet a man who "has given aconite to a half-dozen relatives." Where "no one can sleep for thinking of a money-loving daughter-in-law seduced, of brides that have lost their virtue, of adulterers not out of their 'teens"; where "every street is thronged with gloomy-faced debauchees," and banquets celebrate unnatural and incestuous vice; where spies abound "whose gentle whisper cuts men's throats"; where no woman is decent and no man to be trusted and all wealth dishonestly got and all position attained by abominable means: "The way to be somebody today is to dare some crime."

This is a picture of a very different place from the one through which, a century before, Horace used to make his way to Maecenas. In a hundred years much, no doubt, may happen, and yet the change here is so great one must question if the difference lay wholly in the two Romes and not partly in the two reporters. When Horace wrote he did not have a case to make out—except, of course, on those occasions when his duty as a Roman patriot pressed upon him. But by nature he had no prepossessions which impelled him to emphasize either the bright or the dark, and he looked at human nature very tolerantly. He held up many a one to ridicule and even to scorn; he saw people very seldom as great and good and sometimes as intolerable; he was in no sense an optimist and he knew his Rome through and through. Nevertheless one never closes the book of his satires with a sense that the world of men is detestable. Horace did not find it so. His eyes were as keen to detect the good as the bad, and with all its follies and frailties he liked mankind.

This is the temper of mind which enables a man to estimate truthfully the world around him. It was not Juvenal's. His satires leave one wondering if he ever liked anything, so black and evil as he saw it, was the world he lived in. Whenever he writes, a flood of hate and furious anger fills him and sweeps him away to include everything in his denunciations. He cannot discriminate; all everywhere are abominable and all equally abominable.

His attitude and his method may be seen excellently well in the same satire by which his trustworthiness as a reporter of his own times may be most easily judged, the famous sixth satire. It has been called his "Ballad of Bad Women," but a juster title would be "The Way of All Women," for all women are bad, hateful alike when they chatter Greek and insist on discussing the poets as when they poison their stepsons.

It is far too long an indictment to be given here, but the manner and matter is clear from a mere résumé of the main heads of the first half: What! You who once had your wits are taking a wife—a she-tyrant, when there is rope to be had for a noose? But, says he, he wants a son! And a virtuous woman! O doctors, come and bleed him. Think of that woman who left her husband for a gladiator—of the Empress Messalina's vices. But there—women's lust is the least of their sins. Here's one who brought her husband a fortune—and bought her liberty with her dowry. She can write her love letters under his very nose. This man or that burns with love for his wife. Why? If you shake out the truth, it's her face he loves, not her. Let three wrinkles appear and it's 'Be off. There's another wife coming.' But until then she rules the roost—and her extravagances! Still, suppose a woman could be found, charming, rich, virtuous—could anyone endure to be married to all the perfections? Any wench for my wife rather than you, O mother of the Gracchi. What man was ever so much in love with a woman as not to hate her seven hours out of twelve? Perhaps some faults are small, but they are intolerable to husbands—a woman forever showing off her Greek, for instance. Of course, if you really love your wife, you are lost beyond hope; no woman ever spares the man who loves her. She will arrange your friendships—turn your old friend from your door. 'Crucify that slave,' she cries. 'Why? Give the man a hearing when his life is at stake.' 'Idiot—calling a slave a man. Why? It is my will.' So she lords it—then gets tired of him and finds another husband—eight in five years. Give up all hope of peace, of course, as long as your mother-in-law lives. But in any trouble *cherchez la femme*. Never a case in court in which a woman was not at the bottom of the business. But what can you expect now they've taken to wrestling and fencing? Modesty in a woman like that? Actually panting as she goes through her exercises! Suppose you find her with a lover. Is she ashamed? Listen to the lady: 'We agreed long ago that you were to go your way and

I mine.' Now-a-days a woman eats great oysters at midnight and drinks until the roof spins round. My old friends advise—keep your women at home, under lock and key. Yes—and who will guard the guards? So many varieties and all intolerable: the musical woman ever at an instrument; the one who talks to generals in uniform and can tell you what the Chinese are after; and, worst of all, she who will discuss Virgil and Homer. For heaven's sake, get a wife who doesn't understand all she reads. How I hate a woman who quotes ancient poets to me I never heard of. And all of them plaster their faces with dough and ointments. They will wash them off for company, but when do they want to look nice at home?

And so on and so on for some hundreds of lines more, which include a warning to stepsons in general that "those hot cakes are black with poison of a mother's baking," and end with the statement that you will meet every morning a woman who has murdered her husband—"no street but has its Clytemnestra."

This is a fair sample of the way Juvenal looked at life. The trustworthiness of his entire picture of Rome can be estimated by the trustworthiness of this picture of the women. He hates them so intensely that he loses all sense of perspective, or, more truly, he never had any. Horrible crimes and silly habits are alike damned eternally and whatever happens is the woman's fault. The lady divorced for three wrinkles is a villain, not a victim.

His honesty cannot be questioned. It comes through everything he writes. He is terrifically in earnest, desperately sincere. Certainly he saw all the abominations he says he did, but he was unable, both temperamentally and by reason of his misfortunes, to see anything that was not abominable. His rooted conviction was that the present was *per se* evil and the past good—and the farther off the better. In the last satires, written, he tells us, when that drastic teacher, old age, had taken him in hand, and when the fame of his writings must have softened life's rigors for him, his indignation declines into a milder temper. "How can sad Poverty sing songs?" he wrote in an early satire. "Horace's stomach was well-filled." And certainly in considering the different accounts the two men give of their own times the explanation must have weight. Wrath against one's own wrongs is so easily confused with wrath against the wrongs of the world.

Tacitus, Juvenal's contemporary and a greater writer by far, one of Rome's greatest, also suffered and also saw life as evil chiefly, almost unrelieved. He was not poor like Juvenal; he came of a rich and highly placed family, but the first part of his youth was passed during a time when the condition of the Roman state was as bad as it could well be. He was probably in his early 'teens when Nero was killed, and the atrocities of Nero's last years must have been familiar topics of talk throughout his boyhood. He was grown to manhood when Domitian came to the throne and his best years were over when that monster died. They were years of silence for all except debased flatterers. "Ancient times," wrote Tacitus, "saw the utmost of freedom, we of servitude. Robbed by an inquisition of the common use of speech and hearing, we should have lost our very memory with our voice, were it as much in our power to forget as to be dumb. Now at last [with Domitian's death] our breath has come back, but genius and learning are more easily extinguished than recalled. Fifteen years have been subtracted from our lives, and we are the wretched survivors not only of those taken from us, but of our own selves." In the spirit of these sombre and moving words he writes his history.

The city he takes us into is essentially the same in its moral aspect as Juvenal's city, but it is peopled by politicians and courtiers. Tacitus' world is the great world of the court and the senate, the circles he himself moved in, remote from any Juvenal touched. It is the aristocratic Rome Cicero and Horace knew, but between them and Tacitus is a gulf so wide, it is astounding that they are separated by a mere century or less.

The history of the successors of Augustus, as related by Tacitus, is of men made mad by awful, limitless power. To be the absolute master of the civilized world, to be free in the complete sense of the word, able to indulge every wish the moment it entered the mind, to carry out each caprice no matter how extravagant, to have nothing stand in the way of any desire whatsoever, not a person in all the world, not law, not custom, not religion— the weight of that terrific responsibility was too much for the first men upon whom it fell. Indeed, the fact that during the following century rulers were found who were equal to it shows, better, perhaps, than anything else in Roman history, what the Roman character was capable of at its best. But during the earlier years Tacitus gives us an uninterrupted succession of abominable tyrants. "A black and shameful age," is his summary. "If the narrative in which I am engaged was a record of wars and of men who died in the service of their country, even then the continued disasters would make the reader turn with abhorrence from so many tragic events. How much more from the present subject where we have nothing but base servility and a deluge of blood spilt by a despot in the hour of peace." The base servility was most conspicuous in the case of members of the senate, who, Tacitus says, "tried to see which could be the most obsequious slave. The emperor [Tiberius, in this case, Augustus' heir] was used to say as often as he went from the senate-house, "These men—how ready they are for slavery.'" They descended to incredible depths. At the end of an especially murderous outbreak on the part of Nero, in which Seneca and the poet Lucan lost their lives, when, writes Tacitus, "the city presented a scene of blood, and funerals darkened all the streets," those who had lost their dearest "adorned the emperor's house with laurel and printed kisses on his hand," and a consul-elect moved that "A temple should be built to the Deified Nero, who had risen above the condition of human nature and was entitled to religious worship."

The special horror of the age was the body of informers, Juvenal's spies, "whose gentle whisper cuts men's throats," who, if successful in an accusation, were rewarded with part of the estate of the condemned. So fostered, they spread. "None could trust each other," Tacitus sums up, "not relatives, not friends. The very walls were suspect." The success of this infamy was made easy. People were found guilty on the most frivolous charges, a man killed because he had dreamed he saw the emperor wearing a withered wreath—taken for a bad omen; a woman exiled because "she harbored resentment" on account of a husband's fate; another put to death for weeping over a son's execution. "Natural affection was made a felony and a mother's tear was treason." Many times the accusation was of "secret practices in the magic arts," and with these words classical antiquity and the spirit of enlightenment seem to end; the reader feels suddenly transported to the Middle Ages. "The magic art" would have sounded to Cicero precisely as it does to us.

Within the palace during those years of terror an incredible state of things prevailed. All the emperors died violent deaths, but only after each had murdered those nearest to him. Often their crimes were fantastic, as when Nero put his mother aboard a ship designed so that suddenly in the night it went to pieces, or when the Empress Messalina during the emperor's absence married publicly and with great pomp another man. "It will appear a fabulous tale," Tacitus comments on this last exploit, "but to amuse with fiction is not the design of this work."

Now and again, however, he does amuse, although, of course, without intention. The duel for the possession of Nero between his mother, that truly terrific woman, Agrippina, and the subtle, but even more to be dreaded Poppaea, who became his wife, is a lively narrative. The latter was so fascinating, even Tacitus' austerity softens in describing her: "Virtue excepted, she possessed all the qualities that adorn the female character—the graces of an elegant form, conversation decorated with every winning art, a refined wit. Her favors were bestowed where she saw her interest—a politician in her pleasures." Her methods in detaching Nero from his mother exemplified these traits: "She would make gentle fun of the emperor—call him a pupil under tuition, deprived of personal liberty." Then she would grow serious: "If Agrippina had determined that no one should be her daughter-in-law but a woman the emperor held in detestation, she would herself retire to some remote corner of the earth where she could not see his disgrace." And the words would end in tears. Agrippina with all her violence of character could not hold out against this combination of charm and policy; her death followed.

But before she was removed she had given the state much disquiet. Not because she served poisoned mushrooms to her imperial husband. That, after all, could be accounted a deed within woman's conceded field of action, the home. All that the senate did then was to set upon the throne the son for whom she had committed the murder. But when it came to her taking part in public life, the foundations of Rome rocked. Shortly after Nero's accession, as he was about to give audience to some foreign ambassadors, Agrippina entered and advanced to the tribunal, with the evident intention of taking her seat there and her share in the proceedings. "All who beheld the scene were struck with horror and amazement," says Tacitus. "Seneca alone in the universal confusion had the presence of mind to bid the emperor step forward to greet his mother [as though granting her also an audience]. So, under an appearance of filial respect, the honor of the state was saved."

Juvenal's sixth satire is not the only indication that the men of Rome were beginning to have to defend actively that masculine supremacy which had been, on the whole, so satisfactorily understood in the good days of old.

Side by side with the crimes of violence, and quite as conspicuous, were the crimes of vice. Rome had reached a condition when these did not have to be concealed. Poison still must be administered with some degree of privacy, but scenes of brutal lust were enacted publicly, not only at banquets and great entertainments, but at the spectacles of the games. Tacitus never descends to the arena, but another author of the time makes good this deficiency, Martial, the writer of epigrams. He describes in many a verse what the ampitheatre became under Domitian, when mythological tales of monstrous vice were enacted before the whole city, always, Martial is forever repeating, to the great glory of the one and only lord of all the earth.

To turn from these writers to the Stoics of the same day is like being lifted from a reeking slum or a battlefield heaped with dead to a mountain top or an untrodden shore of the open sea. While Nero was reigning, Seneca from that court red with blood and black with shame, was writing, "We do not need to beg the keeper of a temple to let us approach his idol, God is near you, with you, within you. A holy spirit dwells within us." A few years after Juvenal died, a Caesar of Rome in his soldier's tent on the wild bank of the Danube was solving for himself life's enigma in terms of unselfish duty unflinchingly pursued—"each task from hour to hour performed as though it were to be the last, free from passion, insincerity, self-love, discontent . . . offering to God who is within thee a manly being, a citizen, a soldier at his post, ready to depart from life as soon as the trumpet sounds." And, at the opposite end of the social scale, a man born to a terrible fate, a slave to one of Nero's creatures, had declared not long before that no evil could happen to him because nothing could happen save by the will of God. Then "Let us sing hymns to God and bless him and tell of his benefits."

This is the voice not of philosophy, but of religion. Stoicism from its earliest beginnings was religious. In the fourth century B.C., Zeno, its founder, was preaching in Athens the belief in one supreme God of boundless power and goodness, who was not to be worshipped in temples, unworthy of Deity, but who dwelt in every man, uniting all into one great commonwealth, where there was no distinction between rich or poor, man or woman, bond or free. Three hundred and fifty years later, St. Paul on the Areopagus told the Athenians: "God dwelleth not in temples made with hands. . . . He hath made of one blood all nations of men . . . that they should seek the Lord, if haply they might feel after him and find him, though he be not far from everyone of us: For in him we live and move and have our being." These words are a concise declaration of the Stoic creed, the fundamental tenets of the school.

It must not however be concluded that Stoicism was a religion only and not a philosophy. Zeno had been constrained by the necessity which has pressed upon most of the world's great religious leaders, to attach a rational account of the universe to the intuitive convictions of faith, but his explanation had both of the weaknesses always present when knowledge is sought, not for its own sake, but to prop up something else: it was not very good reason and it was asserted to be infallibly true. As a result, it did not greatly commend itself to the Athenians, intellectualists by nature and trained in the school of Socrates to believe in the dispassionate search for truth and in pursuing it with the Socratic spirit, always remembering that "This may be true, Cratylus. On the other hand, it may very well not be." To fourth-century Athens, belief and rational proof were inextricably connected and the rationality of the proof forever open to re-examination.

A dogmatic theology cannot take root in such soil. Stoicism crossed the Adriatic to find the conditions necessary for its growth.

The Romans were not philosophically minded. Theories of knowledge and of final causes were unimportant and could be accepted without much probing into the basis of truth they rested on. But when the question had to do with the guiding principles needed for life, they knew better than the Greeks what was important. They were men of practical vision: they perceived the struggle between good and evil as the Greeks never did. Pleasure and morality were not seen as opposed to each other in Greece. Socrates visiting a famous courtesan to discover if she was as beautiful as people said, carrying on an agreeable conversation with her, giving her advice how best to attach her lovers to her, leaving

her with a charming compliment to her beauty, is representative
of all Greece. But to the Romans the opposition between duty and
pleasure was absolute. Men's natural inclinations were evil; their
manifest obligation was sternly to control them. Socrates' idea, so
characteristically Greek, that no one can know virtue without
embracing and practicing it—we needs must love the highest
when we see it—was totally inadequate to life's hard demands, as
Romans saw them.

To men so disposed came Stoicism with its final emphasis
upon the will. The Stoic's eyes were fixed on life, not on intellectual truth. Right and wrong had to do not with the reason, but
with the will. All virtue was vain that did not result in virtuous
doing. It was a doctrine fitted to the deepest demands of the
Roman nature. They wanted not philosophy, which is for understanding, but religion, which is for action. "We are the most religious of all nations," wrote Cicero, and when religion is seen as a
force to make men better, not to explain the universe, his words
are true. It was in Rome that the conquest of Christianity was
most complete, and it was from Rome that the Christianizing of
the world proceeded. The fact is easily comprehensible when the
Roman genius for religion is perceived—religion as it is understood by the west, the power of the good to conquer the evil.

The Christian Church never proclaimed in stronger terms the
all-sufficiency of this power than the Stoics did. Whoever recognized the divine light within him and strove to keep it bright,
was removed from the possibility of evil. Pain, sorrow, death,
could not enter that inner shrine. It was the impregnable citadel
where peace reigned, no matter what was without. Epictetus, a
slave who knew the horrors of Nero's court, felt himself free in his
slavery and independent of all men could do to him. "Suppose the
tyrant says he will throw me into prison—my spirit cannot be
imprisoned. 'But I can put you to death.' 'No—You can only cut
off my head.'" The only thing that matters is a will bent upon the
good, and this is wholly within a man's own mastery. That alone

is our concern. Our lot in life, slave or emperor, God assigns. All
we have to do is to play well the part he gives us, as the actor does,
whatever the rôle he is cast for. Outside success and failure are of
no consequence. "Virtue consists in aiming at the mark, not hit-
ting it." The man who tries hardest is thereby the most successful.
The wise man of the Stoics' ideal is like the good athlete who
strives to the utmost, but to play the game, not to win it.

The power there is in an ideal to bring about its own reality
was exemplified many a time in those last days of Rome. In the
city where Tacitus and Juvenal saw public exhibitions of unnam-
able vice, the Stoics lived lives of austere purity. To them all sex-
ual relations outside of marriage were "disgraceful by reason of
their lawlessness and foulness." They held—it is an instance of
their astonishing modernity—the equality of man and woman,
and conceded no more license to the one than to the other. "Do
you allow to the master of the house an intrigue with his slave-
woman?" they asked. "Then, of course, you allow the mistress to
consort with her man-slave? No? Yet you hold a man superior to
a woman? Less able, then, to restrain his desires? Your position,
you see, is untenable. If men claim superiority to women, they
must show themselves superior in self-control."

In an age of cruelty, widespread as it never was to be again, the
Stoics declared the cruel man to be possessed by "a dreadful disease of the mind" which reached "the extreme of insanity when
pleasure was felt in watching a human being die." Alone in the
Roman world their voice was heard denouncing the centuries-old
gladiatorial games.

They were alone, too, in teaching that a slave was to be treated
as a human being. This insistence was the logical result of their
belief in "the true Light, which lighteth every man that cometh
into the world." Master and slave, by virtue of this sharing in
common, became each a brother to the other. Perhaps it was here
that their attitude stood out in sharpest contrast to that of their
age. Rome saw in those days four hundred slaves at once led forth

to die, men and women, young and old, because their master had
been killed by one of them. The murderer was known, and even
the brutal crowd in the streets was softened to pity at the sight of
so many innocent people about to suffer death. But the senate
refused mercy; an illustrious member stated that "those we have
in our service are the scum of humanity collected from all quarters
of the globe," and that the only way to keep them subject was to
keep them in terror.

Precisely at this time Seneca was writing: "'They are slaves,'
people declare. Nay, they are men. Slaves? No, comrades." Epictetus followed, declaring that a slave is "your brother, who is sprung
from God . . . of the same heavenly descent as you." The principle
which became fundamental in Roman law, that all men are by
nature equal, was derived, the historians agree, from the Stoics,
and if Stoicism had no other claim to admiration, that alone
would set it high among the great beneficent activities of the
world.

How widespread the Stoics were is not known, but it is gener-
ally agreed that their numbers were large. If so, the fact speaks
volumes for the strength of the Roman character, for Stoicism was
a religion for the strong. It did not teach the practice of virtue as
a means to eternal bliss, still less as a means to escape eternal misery. Tales, Seneca says, which represent the other world as terrible,
are fiction. "There is no black darkness awaiting the dead, no lake
of fire, . . . no renewal of the reign of tyrants." The Stoics fixed
their attention on this earthly life. Goodness, here and now, was
enough. The good man was the happy man whatever befell him,
in death as in life. It was Seneca who said, "Virtue is its own
reward." The Stoic asked for no other.

But always, consoling and strengthening, there was the consciousness of a divine presence and a divine purpose. "When you
have shut your door and darkened your room," says Epictetus,
"say not that you are alone. God is in your room." And Seneca
writes: "God does not leave a good man in prosperity. He tries

him, he strengthens him, he prepares him for himself." Therefore, knowing there is a purpose behind all, "I do not obey God—I agree with him. I follow him heart and soul, not because I must." "Is it God's will," asks Epictetus, "that I shall have a fever? It is my will too." And, as regards death, "To have God for our maker, father, guardian, should not that free us from all sadness and from all fear?" "Serenely take your leave," Marcus Aurelius writes, "serene as he who gives you your discharge."

So in latter-day Rome religion at its noblest confronted the utmost of depravity. The two streams seem not to have intermingled. The debased were not raised to a higher level by the presence among them of the great and good, and in the midst of vilest evil the Stoics never lowered their standard. Rome was a divided city, separated by a final division which cut deeper still than the old opposition between millionaire and pauper, autocrat and slave. Absolute good and absolute evil were arrayed against each other, with no conception of a principle of mediation between them. Vice was content, virtue too. The Stoic's creed armed the good man invulnerably against evil; it did not enlist him for active warfare upon the evil. The final view of ancient Rome given by her last great writers is of a state that has come to an inevitable standstill; progress is not possible.

XIII

The End of Antiquity

Throughout the great days of the early Republic as they have come down to us in Polybius, in Livy, in Plutarch, in many an allusion in other writers, Rome was a nation perpetually at war. By the time Plautus was born she was absolute mistress of Italy, but the achievement took some five hundred years of fighting. Terence had been dead only a short time when the last Punic War made the Mediterranean a Roman sea. The east called next to the ever-moving, ever-growing power, and Cicero, fighting in Cilicia, was one of its instruments in extending Roman dominion far into Asia. Julius Caesar conquered the west and made Northern Africa a province of the empire. Horace's Rome was mistress from the Sahara to the Rhine and the Danube, from the Euphrates to the Atlantic.

"Keep the empire within its bounds" was the maxim Augustus bequeathed to his successors. The eight-hundred-years war of conquest was ended. The pioneer work of advancing against constantly opposing physical forces cannot in the nature of things go on forever. That task Rome had now completed. She had accomplished marvels; she had made the framework for a new world. A mightier task by far remained: to keep pace intellectually and spiritually with the enormous material advance, so as to be able to plan and build the new construction which the new framework demanded. A vision and an understanding not needed before were now imperatively called for.

Caesar, it is possible, had both requisites and could have rebuilt the state, but Rome did not see that the old world had passed away, and he died in consequence. Augustus, taught by what Caesar had begun, understood the immediate needs of the present and established a system which worked efficiently for some centuries. But these two were Rome's only great constructive statesmen in her latter years. No other men were able to go forward with the march of events and meet new conditions with new provisions. On the contrary, all turned unanimously for help to the days of old. Go back to the virtues of our forefathers, the patriots cried, from Cicero on to the last martyrs for liberty in Tacitus' pages. The longing voiced by the whole of Latin literature is for a return to the times when Rome was simple and pious and able to bear hardship. All that men were able to do when confronted with difficulties such as never had been known before, was to look to the past, which always seems so good, so comprehensible, and try to apply to the baffling present the solutions of a life that was outgrown.

The old virtues were completely inadequate for the new day. The abilities of the pioneer and the conqueror, which had made the empire, could not meet the conditions which resulted from their achievements. To overcome nature or nations calls for one set of qualities; to use the victory as a basis for a better state in human affairs calls for another. When men must turn from extending their possessions to making wise use of them, audacity, self-reliance, endurance, are not enough. Individualism, whether of the road-builder in the wilderness or of the self-determined general in the field, must give way. It is suited only to the wilderness and the battlefield. After Rome's great victories had been won, the fruits of them could be gathered only by men working together. She had reached a point in her development when the good of the whole was bound up with the good of each man and the good of each man was bound up with the good of the whole, and the problem of achieving it was complicated far beyond the

simple virtues of the simple man. Her first necessity was for intellectual and spiritual insight, for wisdom and disinterestedness.

What Rome was capable of, the achievement of her empire
shows. The Roman character had great qualities, great potential
strength. If the people had held together, realizing their interde-
pendence and working for a common good, their problems, completely strange and enormously difficult though they were, would
not, it may well be believed, have proved too much for them. But
they were split into sharpest oppositions, extremes that ever grew
more extreme and so more irresponsible. A narrow selfishness
kept men blind when their own self-preservation demanded a
world-wide outlook.

History repeats itself. The fact is a testimony to human stupidity. The saying has become a truism; nevertheless, the study of the
past is relegated to the scholar and the school-boy. And yet it is
really a chart for our guidance—no less than that. Where we now
are going astray and losing ourselves, other men once did the
same, and they left a record of the blind alleys they went down.
We are like youth that can never learn from age—but youth is
young, and wisdom is for the mature. We that are grown should
not find it impossible to learn from the ages-old recorded experience of the past.

Our mechanical and industrial age is the only material
achievement that can be compared with Rome's during the two
thousand years in between. It is worth our while to perceive that
the final reason for Rome's defeat was the failure of mind and
spirit to rise to a new and great opportunity, to meet the challenge
of new and great events. Material development outstripped
human development; the Dark Ages took possession of Europe,
and classical antiquity ended.

CHRONOLOGY

753 B.C	Traditional date of founding of Rome.
266	Conquest of Italy to the Rubicon completed.
264–241	First Punic War.
218–201	Second Punic War.
184	Plautus died.
185–159	Traditional dates for Terence's birth and death.
167	Polybius brought to Rome.
149–146	Third Punic War and destruction of Carthage.
133–121	Tiberius and Caius Gracchus agitate reforms.
106	Cicero born.
102 or 100	Caesar born.
87	Catullus said to have been born; date uncertain.
82	Sulla dictator.
78	Sulla's death.
70	Virgil born.
65	Horace born.
63	Conspiracy of Catiline.
60	First Triumvirate—Caesar, Pompey, Crassus.
59	Livy born.
58–51	Conquest of Gaul by Caesar.
57	Catullus died. Again date conjectural.
49	War between Caesar and Pompey.
48	Pompey defeated at Pharsalus, flees to Egypt and there murdered.
44	Assassination of Caesar.
43	Second Triumvirate—Octavius (Augustus), Antony, Lepidus. Cicero killed.
42	Battle of Philippi. Death of Brutus and Cassius.
31	Defeat of Antony in battle of Actium. Augustus

	sole ruler of empire.
30	Death of Antony and Cleopatra.
19	Virgil's death.
8	Horace's death.
3(?)	Seneca born.
14 A.D.	Death of Augustus.
17	Livy's death.
14–37	Reign of Tiberius—extended law against high treason to include most trivial matters. Rewards given to informers. Suffocated when near death.
37–41	Caius (Caligula). At least half crazy. Murdered by soldiers.
41–54	Claudius, married Messalina, then Agrippina, who poisoned him after he had adopted her son, Nero. Tacitus probably born toward end of his reign.
54–68	Nero. Fled from uprising against him and killed himself just as soldiers arrived to execute him. End of the house of Caesar.
65	Seneca died by order of Nero.
69	The "Year of Three Emperors": Galba, killed by uprising of soldiers; Otho, killed himself after being defeated by Vitellius, who was in his turn killed by uprising of soldiers.
69–79	Vespasian. Good administrator. Capture of Jerusalem. Coliseum built. Vespasian succeeded by son.
79–81	Titus. Destruction of Herculaneum and Pompeii. Succeeded by his brother.
81–96	Domitian. Murdered by his freedman and his wife.
96–180	The "Five Good Emperors": Nerva, Trajan, Hadrian, Antoninus Pius, Marcus Aurelius, each, from Nerva on, adopted by his predecessor.

Tacitus probably died during Trajan's reign, around 117.

Juvenal known to be writing during Domitian's reign and probably died in Hadrian's reign, around 135.

Epictetus born probably around 50 and died probably early in second century.

REFERENCES

PAGE *Line*

62   13   *Ad Att.* IV, 17. All quotations from Cicero's letters are taken from the admirable translation in the Loeb Classical Library.

63   3   Plutarch, *Caes.* According to Plutarch, Clodius was discovered, but Cicero says not.

65   1   *Ad Att.* I, 16.

66   33   *Q. Fr.* III, 9.

67   7   *Ad Att.* II, 95.

70   27   *Ad Att.* II, 15.

71   1   *Ad Att.* XII, 9.

72   12   Ib., VII, 8.

72   17   Ib., II, 25.

72   24   Ib., I, 14.

72   32   *Ad Fam.* IX, 16.

73   4   *Ad Att.* II, 25.

73   7   Ib., II, 19.

73   21   Ib., XIV, 18.

73   32   Ib., XIV, 13.

74   7   Ib., XIV, 9.

74   33   Ib., VI, 9.

75   18   Ib., I, 8.

75   24   *Q. Fr.* III, 1.

76   8   *Ad Att.* IV, 4*a*.

76   17   *Ad Fam.* VII, 1.

77   6   Ib., VIII, 14.

77   17   *Ad Att.* VI, 1.

77   25   *Ad Fam.* IX, 22.

77   33   Ib., IX, 26.

PAGE *Line*

78	10	Ib., IX, 20.
78	17	Ib., XIV, 1.
78	24	Ib., XIV, 20.
78	30	*Ad Att.* XII, 32.
79	9	*Ad Fam.* IV, 6.
79	13	*Ad Att.* IV, 18.
79	22	*Ad Fam.* VIII, 1.
79	23	Ib., VIII, 14.
79	32	*Ad Att.* VII, 5.
80	4	*Ad Fam.* VIII, 15.
80	10	*Ad Att.* VIII, 9.
80	11	Ib., VII, 1.
80	24	Ib., X, 8*b*.
80	32	Ib., IX, 18.
81	1	Ib., IX, 7*c*.
81	5	*Ad Fam.* IV, 4.
81	13	*Ad Att.* XIII, 5.
82	17	Ib., XIII, 52.
83	3	Ib., XIV, 21.
84	12	Ib., XIV, 17.
84	17	*De Off.* II, 24.
84	22	*Ad Att.* VIII, 11.
84	29	*Conivr. Cat.* 51*ff.*
85	1	*Ad Att.* VII, 2.
85	28	Catullus XXIX.
86	9	Catullus LVII.
86	20	Plutarch *Caes.* IX.
86	30	Suet. *Oct.* 45.
87	7	Plutarch *Cic.* XVIII.
87	15	Plut. *Caes.* III, also Suet. *Caes.* I.
87	22	*Ad Att.* II, 17.
87	30	Ib., IX, 10.
88	1	Ib., XV, 26.
88	11	Ib., XV, 11.
88	27	Ib., XV, 12.
89	13	Ib., XVI, 11.
89	26	*Ad Fam.* IX, 20.
90	10	*Ad Att.* XV, 15.

PAGE *Line*
90 15 *Caes.* B. G. II end
90 27 Ib., I, 38.
91 14 *Ad Fam.* VII, 15.
91 20 *De Am.* XXIII.
91 24 *Ad Fam.* XVI, 5, 6.
92 3 *Ad Att.* II, 9.
94 5 Ib., II, 18.
95 23 Ib., II, 20.
95 26 *Ad Att.* IX, 10.
96 2 *Ad Fam.* VII, 5.
96 30 *Ad Att.* XII, 15.
97 24 Ib., XVI, 15.
98 17 Ib., X, 10.
99 7 *Ad Fam.* VIII, 1.
99 16 *Ad Att.* III, 8.
100 2 Ib., VI, 2.
103 19 *Pro Cael.* II, 1*ff.*
109 11 Cat. II.
110 1 Ib., III.
110 22 Ib., LXXXVI.
111 1 Ib., V.
111 17 Ib., LXXXIII.
111 28 Ib., XCII.
112 5 Ib., CIX.
113 1 Ib., LXVIII*b*.
113 23 Ib., LXXXV.
113 28 Ib., LXX.
114 2 Ib., LXXII.
114 16 Ib., LXXV.
114 25 Ib., VIII.
115 27 Ib., CI.
116 26 Ib., CVII.
117 5 Ib., LXXVI.
118 1 Ib., LVIII.
121 33 *Serm.* II, 1, 1.
128 25 *Carm.* IV, 2, 5, 25.
129 2 Ib., III, 30.
129 25 *Serm.* I, 6, 115.
130 17 Ib., II, 6, 1.

PAGE *Line*
130 21 *Carm.* II, 18, 1.
130 25 Ib., I, 31.
131 31 *Ep.* I, 18, 106.
133 33 *Carm.* III, 6, 16.
134 3 Ib., III, 15, 1.
134 7 Ib., III, 4, 65.
134 10 Ib., III, 5, 46.
135 12 *Ep.* I, 6, 6.
135 13 Ib., II, 2, 180.
135 30 *Ser.* II, 6, 27.
136 14 *Ep.* II, 2, 72.
137 11 *Ep.* I, 6, 37.
138 8 Ib., I, 17 and 18.
139 27 *Serm.* II, 3, 151.
140 1 Ib., II, 3, 94.
140 9 But Aristophanes shows the fashion is beginning: *Wasps* 1212
140 21 *Ser.* II, 2, 26.
140 33 Ib., II, 8 and 4.
141 17 *Ser.* II, 76.
141 28 *Ep.* I, 5, 22.
142 22 *Serm.* I, 5, 51.
143 27 Ib., II, 6, 73.
144 14 *Serm.* II, 6, 44.
144 19 Ib., I, 3, 81.
144 24 Ib., I, 3, 10.
145 34 Ib., II, 6, 65.
147 6 *Ep.* II, 1, 185.
148 1 *Aen.* I, 278.
149 21 Lucian, Demonax 57 (quoted by Magnin, *Origines du Théatre*).
149 24 *Philostr. Apollon.* vit. IV, 22 (Magnin, *op. cit.*).
149 28 Xiph. LXIX, 8.
149 29 Suet. *Tit.* 7.
149 33 Mart. VIII, 26.
150 11 Xiph. LXVIII, 8.
150 13 Mart. I, 6.
150 14 Xiph. LXXII, 22.
150 21 Suet. *Claud.* 21.

PAGE *Line*
150 29 Lactant. *De Mort. Pers.* 21 (quoted by Magnin, *op. cit.*).
161 5 *Noct. Att.* XVII, 8.
164 21 Ib., XVII, 7.
165 4 *Georg.* I, 1.
165 21 Ib., II, 323.
166 9 Ib., III, 440*ff.*
166 16 Ib., 235.
167 11 *Iliad,* XVIII, 370.
167 21 *Aen.* VIII, 415.
168 28 *Iliad,* III, 399.
169 9 *Aen.* IV, 1.
169 11 Ib., 75.
169 15 Ib., 80.
169 16 Ib., 129*ff.*
170 7 Ib., 314.
170 19 *Odys.* IV, 120.
173 23 *Aen.* I, 92.
173 25 *Odys.* V, 306.
174 5 *Aen.* VI, 823.
178 25 Eurip., *Troiad,* 98 (Gilbert Murray, tr.).
179 7 Sen. *Troad,* 1*ff.*
179 28 Eurip., *op. cit.,* 632.
180 3 Ib., 288.
180 8 Sen., *op. cit.,* 62.
180 13 Eurip., *op. cit.,* 725.
181 3 Eurip., *op. cit.,* 740.
181 17 Sen., *op. cit.,* 419.
182 12 Eurip., *op. cit.,* 1173.
186 21 There are only three personal references.
       Sat. III, 319; XI, 65; XV, 45.
186 28 Sat. V, 80.
187 7 Ib., VII, 150, 222.
187 28 Ib., X, 26.
187 29 Ib., I, 71.
187 31 Ib., 155.
187 31 Ib., 77.
187 34 Ib., II, 8.
188 1 Ib., II, 132.

PAGE *Line*

188	2	Ib., IV, 110.
188	5	Ib., I, 73.
191	1	Ib., VII, 62.
191	17	Agric. VIII.
192	13	Ann. III, 65.
192	27	Ib., XV, 71.
192	30	Ib., 74.
193	2	Ib., IV, 69.
193	19	Ib., XIV, 5.
193	21	Ib., XI, 26.
193	30	Ib., XIII, 71.
194	1	Ib., XIV, 1.
194	20	Ib., XIII, 5.
195	12	Sen. *Ep.* 41, 5.
195	17	*Marc. Aur.* II, 5.
195	25	Epict. *Disc.* I, 16.
198	16	Condensed from Stob III, 6, 23 (quoted by Arnold, *Roman Stoicism*).
198	24	Sen. *Clem.* I, 25, 3.
199	1	Tac. *Ann.* XIV, 42.
199	10	Sen. *Ep.* VI, 47.
199	25	Sen. *Dial.* VI, 19, 4.
200	1	Ib., I, 4, 7.
200	3	Sen. *Ep.* 96, 2.
200	5	Epict. *Disc.* IV, 1, 89 (quoted by Arnold, *op. cit.*).
200	6	*Arrian* Epict. I, 9.